A Spiritual Journey
Life Renewal Devotional

A
Spiritual
Journey
Life
Renewal
Devotional

*Daily Reflections
from the Bible
and People of Faith*

Wightman Weese, editor

Tyndale House Publishers, Inc.,
Wheaton, Illinois

Library of Congress Cataloging-in-Publication Data
A Spiritual journey life renewal devotional : daily reflections from
the Bible and people of faith / Wightman Weese, editor.
    p.   cm.
  Includes bibliographical references.
  ISBN 0-8423-5931-1
  1. Devotional calendars.   2. Spiritual life—Christianity.
I. Weese, Wightman
BV4811.S63   1993
242'.2—dc20   93-22492

Printed in the United States of America

99   98   97   96   95   94   93
8   7   6   5   4   3   2   1

CONTENTS

The Spiritual Journey

The Christian life being described as a pilgrimage or a lifelong journey is an idea that has been bound up in the minds of Christians throughout the centuries. The goal was described as a "Celestial City," by John Bunyan in his *Pilgrim's Progress*. Several passages in the Scriptures also lend to this notion. Both the apostle Paul and the writer of Hebrews called it "a race well run."

Of one truth we can be sure—the Christian life can't be experienced at a standstill. We either move forward or we lose ground. It is either progress or regression; we either ascend to celestial heights or sink in spiritual declension. Choices about the journey are made each day—every day.

Spiritual life can begin as easily as our natural birth, and birth is what God called it—spiritual birth. But spiritual growth, like physical growth, requires careful nurture and self-discipline. For that we need help from God and from his servants sent to encourage us along the way.

Spiritual giants, from Clement of Rome and Augustine of Hippo to Warren Wiersbe and A. W. Tozer, have felt the influence of the world and the pull of heaven. In this book we have searched through their writings for their secrets about the journey. Saintly women, Madame Guyon, Jessie Penn-Lewis, Hannah Whitall Smith, and others offer light for our path as we journey together.

The way we run the race, how we follow the pilgrim road, is as important as the destination we seek. It is as easy as loving God himself and as hard as loving our neighbors—the kind and good ones along with the unkind and evil ones. It is as easy as saying yes to God but as difficult as saying no to all the sinful attractions confronting us along the pathway. Both the challenge and the strength for the journey come from God himself. The secret is in *knowing* God, not *knowing about* God, and to help you know God better is the primary purpose of this book.

Fifty-two undated sections, each containing seven readings, provide a year's devotional reading that you can start at any time. May this book add spiritual enrichment to you for each step of the way.

THE JOURNEY BEGINS

*The world was not worthy of them.
They wandered in deserts and
mountains, and in caves and holes in
the ground. These were all commended
for their faith, yet none of them
received what had been promised.
God had planned something better for
us so that only together with us
would they be made perfect.*

(HEBREWS 11:38-40)

As believers, we travel through alien territory, seeking higher ground, more excellent light, deeper relationship with God. The delightful news is that our journey begins whenever we choose to begin. Our Great Shepherd, the Guide, beckons us. "Follow me."

Venture forth on the long journey home

Blessed are those whose strength is in you, who have set their hearts on pilgrimage.
(PSALM 84:5)

Every one that comes to Christ has a journey to perform in this world. Some have a long, and some a short one. It is through a wilderness. Still Christ prays that at the end you may be with him. Every one that comes to Christ hath his twelve hours to fill up for Christ. "I must work the works of him that sent me, while it is day." But when that is done, Christ prays that you may be with him. He means that you shall come to his Father's house with him. . . . You are never very intimate with a person till you see them in their own house—till you know them at home. This is what Christ wants with us— that we shall come to be with him, at his own home. He wants us to come to the same Father's bosom with him: "I ascend to My Father and your Father."

Robert Murray McCheyne

Seek out the well-marked trail

Whether you turn to the right or to the left,
your ears will hear a voice behind you, saying,
"This is the way; walk in it."
(ISAIAH 30:21)

Whatever awaits us is encountered first by him—
each difficulty and complication; each wild beast or
wilder robber; each yawning chasm or precipitous
path. . . . Bind this comfort to your heart: that the
Savior has tried for himself all the experiences
through which he asks you to pass; and he would not
ask you to pass through them unless he was sure that
they were not too difficult for your feet, or too
trying for your strength. . . . This is the blessed
life—not anxious to see far in front; not careful
about the next step; not eager to choose the path;
not weighted with the heavy responsibilities of the
future: but quietly following behind the Shepherd,
one step at a time.

F. B. Meyer

1.2

Proceed along our
heaven-prepared course

So on that day Moses swore to me,
"The land on which your feet have walked will
be your inheritance and that of your children
forever, because you have followed the
LORD my God wholeheartedly."
(JOSHUA 14:9)

Let us mind our own faults, and not trouble ourselves about those of other people. For those who live carefully regulated lives are apt to be shocked at everything, yet we might well learn very important lessons from those who shock us. True, our outward demeanor and behavior may appear better than theirs, but this, although good, is not the most important thing. We should not expect everyone else to travel along our own road, and we should not attempt to point out to them the spiritual path when perhaps we do not know it ourselves.

Teresa of Avila

Follow the well-lit path

If we claim to have fellowship with him yet walk in the darkness, we lie and do not live by the truth. But if we walk in the light, as he is in the light, we have fellowship with one another, and the blood of Jesus, his Son, purifies us from all sin.
(1 JOHN 1:6-7)

For the Way of Light . . . a man who would make the pilgrimage to his appointed home must put his whole heart into his work. To aid our steps on the road, illumination has been given to us then—Love your Maker; fear your Creator; give glory to him who redeemed you from death. Practice singleness of heart, and a richness of spirit. Shun the company of those who walk in the Way of Death. Abhor anything that is displeasing to God, and hold every form of hypocrisy in detestation. Be sure that you never depart from the commandments of the Lord.

Barnabas

Take the long-range view

This is what the LORD says: "Stand at the crossroads and look; ask for the ancient paths, ask where the good way is, and walk in it, and you will find rest for your souls."
(JEREMIAH 6:16)

Of all that can be thought or said about God, his infinitude is the most difficult to grasp. . . . Yet we must try, for the Holy Scriptures teach that God is infinite and, if we accept his other attributes, we must of necessity accept this one too. From the effort to understand, we must not turn back because the way is difficult and there are no mechanical aids for the ascent. The view is better farther up and the journey is not one for the feet but for the heart. Let us seek, therefore, such "traces of thought and mountings of the mind" as God may be pleased to grant us, knowing that the Lord often pours eyesight on the blind and whispers to babes and sucklings truths never dreamed of by the wise and prudent.

A. W. Tozer

1.5

Seek a better world

*For he was looking forward to the city with
foundations, whose architect and builder is God.*
(Hebrews 11:10)

Perhaps it will be asked, should we think as much
and as often about spiritual things as about the
lawful things of this life? To that I say we should, and
more and *more often,* if we are to be truly spiritually
minded. What would you think of a person who
pretends that he is journeying to another country
where he has an inheritance and yet whose whole
conversation is about the trifling things he has to
leave behind when he goes? The Saviour forbids us
to be anxious about the things of this life, as though
our heavenly Father could not care for us. Nor
should the things of this life occupy our thoughts as
fully as spiritual things (Matthew 6:31-33).

John Owen

Keep the pace

Therefore, since we are surrounded by such a great cloud of witnesses, let us throw off everything that hinders and the sin that so easily entangles, and let us run with perseverance the race marked out for us.

(HEBREWS 12:1)

Let us . . . for the love of God, encourage ourselves to go on, and leave our reasons and our fears in his hands. Let us forget this natural weakness which occupies us so readily. . . . Our only task is to journey on with good speed so that we may see the Lord. Although we may get few or no comforts here, we shall be making a big mistake if we worry about our health, especially as it will not be improved by further anxiety over it. That I know from my own experience. I also know that our progress has nothing to do with the body, which is the thing that matters least of all. The journey about which I am referring demands great humility, and it is the lack of it that will prevent us from making progress.

Teresa of Avila

THE MIND-SET FOR THE JOURNEY

*Let us fix our eyes on Jesus, the author
and perfecter of our faith, who for the
joy set before him endured the cross,
scorning its shame, and sat down at the
right hand of the throne of God.*

(HEBREWS 12:2)

Leave your fears behind

Where is the man who fears the Lord? God will teach him how to choose the best.
(PSALM 25:12, TLB)

The infinite heart of the infinite God flows out in love towards our Lord Jesus Christ. And there is no fear in the bosom of Christ. All his fears are past. Once he said, "While I suffer thy terrors I am distressed"; but now he is in perfect love, and perfect love casteth out fear. Hearken, trembling souls! Here you may find rest to your souls. You do not need to live another hour under your tormenting fears. Jesus Christ has borne the wrath of which you are afraid. He now stands a refuge for the oppressed—a refuge in the time of trouble. Look to Christ, and you will find rest. Call upon the name of the Lord, and you will be delivered.

Robert Murray McCheyne

Enjoy the journey with Christ

*Consider him who endured such opposition
from sinful men, so that you will
not grow weary and lose heart.*
(HEBREWS 12:3)

Our peace with God depends on what Christ has done for us. We love him for that. But more; we rejoice that he is now so glorious in heaven. We look forward to being with him, but we will not enjoy being with him there if we do not enjoy being with him here. I know some people who are anxious if too long a time passes without having him in their thoughts. Sadly I know more who rarely have him in their thoughts. It is important to think about Christ in a biblical way. . . . We must make sure that the means we use to help us meditate are themselves spiritual. Pray continually for the Holy Spirit's help. Read some passage of Scripture which teaches something about Christ, and think about that.

John Owen

Await the return of the Beloved

In a moment of anger I turned my face a little while; but with everlasting love I will have pity on you, says the Lord, your Redeemer.
(ISAIAH 54:8, TLB)

Although God has no other desire than to impart himself to you, he frequently conceals himself for a purpose. It may be to arouse you from laziness, or perhaps you have not been seeking him in faith and love. But, for whatever reason, he does so out of his abundant goodness and faithfulness to you. Often these apparent withdrawings of himself are succeeded by the caresses of his love. During these seasons, you will begin to believe that the way to prove your faith is by a greater degree of affection or by an exertion of strength and activity. Surely, you may say, this will induce God to revisit you. No, dear soul, believe me, this is not the way. You must await the return of the Beloved with patient love, humility, peace, and silent worship.

Jeanne Guyon

Keep your mind fixed on him

But Abraham never doubted. He believed God,
for his faith and trust grew ever stronger,
and he praised God for this blessing
even before it happened.
(ROMANS 4:20, TLB)

Those who mind Christ's glory, he mindeth their salvation. He is interceding for you in heaven when you are glorifying him on earth; he is doing your business in heaven when you are doing his business in the world; he is your advocate, and you are his bailiffs and factors: Matthew 10:32, "Whosoever shall confess me before men, him will I confess also before my Father which is in heaven." When you own Christ in the world, and avow his name and truth in the world, you shall lose nothing. When you come to pray, Christ will own you: Father, hear him, this is one of mine. You cannot honor Christ so much as he will honor you.

Thomas Manton

Maintain an attitude of prayer

Your life is now hidden with Christ in God.
(COLOSSIANS 3:3)

There is a way of life so hid with Christ in God that in the midst of the day's business one is inwardly lifting brief prayers, short ejaculations of praise, subdued whispers of adoration and of tender love to the Beyond that is within. No one need know about it. I only speak to you because it is a sacred trust, not mine but to be given to others. One can live in a well-nigh continuous state of unworded prayer, directed toward God, directed toward people and enterprises we have on our heart. There is no hurry about it all; it is a life unspeakable and full of glory, an inner world of splendor within which we, unworthy, may live. Some of you know it and live in it; others of you may wistfully long for it; it can be yours.

Thomas R. Kelly

Count on his presence

And this is the will of God, that I
should not lose even one of all those
he has given me, but that I should raise them
to eternal life at the Last Day.
(JOHN 6:39, TLB)

We have Christ always for us in heaven; he hath a part of his office to perform there. His absence doth not hinder us from having a right to him, or a spiritual possession of him. He is ours, and he hath his residence in heaven, and hath power to open it to us and give us entrance. His high honor doth not hinder him from the discharge of his office to do us good. He is at God's right hand, and yet a minister of the sanctuary. . . . Many forget their poor friends when advanced; Christ regardeth his poor church as much as ever. . . . Hebrews 4:15, "We have not a high priest which cannot be touched with the feeling of our infirmities." His heart is not changed by his honor; but he is in a greater capacity to do us good.

Thomas Manton

Wear his insignia proudly

If we think that our present service for him is hard, just remember that some day we are going to sit with him and rule with him. But if we give up when we suffer, and turn against Christ, then he must turn against us.

(2 TIMOTHY 2:12, TLB)

All things must come to an end, and there are two alternatives before us. They are life and death; and every one of us will have to go to his own particular place. There are two different coinages, so to speak, in circulation, God's and the world's, each with its own distinctive marking. Unbelievers carry the stamp of the world; while the faithful in love bear the stamp of God the Father, through Jesus Christ. Unless we are ready and willing to die in conformity with his Passion, his life is not in us.

Ignatius of Antioch

God Wants to Be with Us

*Remember how the LORD your God led
you all the way in the desert these forty
years, to humble you and to test you
in order to know what was in your
heart, whether or not you
would keep his commands.*

(DEUTERONOMY 8:2)

The Guide is easy to recognize

*I am the good shepherd; I know my sheep
and my sheep know me—just as the Father
knows me and I know the Father—
and I lay down my life for the sheep.*
(JOHN 10:14-15)

Always, everywhere God is present, and always he
seeks to discover himself. To each one he would
reveal not only that he is, but what he is as well. He
did not have to be persuaded to discover himself to
Moses. "And the Lord descended in the cloud, and
stood with him there, and proclaimed the name of
the Lord." He not only made a verbal proclamation
of his nature but he revealed his very self to Moses
so that the skin of Moses' face shone with the
supernatural light. It will be a great moment for
some of us when we begin to believe that God's
promise of self-revelation is literally true: that he
promised much, but promised no more than he
intends to fulfill.

A. W. Tozer

We need never wonder where he is

When I come back to life again,
you will know that I am in my Father,
and you in me, and I in you.
(JOHN 14:20, TLB)

Our pursuit of God is successful just because he is forever seeking to manifest himself to us. The revelation of God to any man is not God coming from a distance upon a time to pay a brief and momentous visit to the man's soul. Thus to think of it is to misunderstand it all. The approach of God to the soul or of the soul to God is not to be thought of in spatial terms at all. There is no idea of physical distance involved in the concept. It is not a matter of miles, but experience. To speak of being near to or far from God is to use language in a sense always understood when applied to our ordinary human relationships. . . . We need never shout across the spaces to an absent God. He is nearer than our own soul, closer than our most secret thoughts.

A. W. Tozer

3.2

Fill your mind with a divine vision

When I first came to you I didn't use lofty words and brilliant ideas to tell you God's message. For I decided that I would speak only of Jesus Christ and his death on the cross.
(1 CORINTHIANS 2:1-2, TLB)

We console ourselves with the knowledge that it is God himself who puts it in our hearts to seek him and makes it possible in some measure to know him, and he is pleased with even the feeblest effort to make him known. If some watcher or holy one who has spent his glad centuries by the sea of fire were to come to earth, how meaningless to him would be the ceaseless chatter of the busy tribes of men. . . . And were such a one to speak on earth would he not speak of God? Would he not charm and fascinate his hearers with rapturous descriptions of the Godhead? And after hearing him could we ever again consent to listen to anything less than theology, the doctrine of God?

A. W. Tozer

Know the One to whom we should be grateful

When he sees all that is accomplished by the anguish of his soul, he shall be satisfied; and because of what he has experienced, my righteous Servant shall make many to be counted righteous before God, for he shall bear all their sins.

(ISAIAH 53:11, TLB)

Bear in mind, then, O children of joy, that there is not a single thing which the Lord in his goodness has not made clear to us beforehand, so that we may know to whom all our thanks and praises are due. Though the Son of God was the divine Lord, and the future Judge of living and dead alike, yet nevertheless he suffered, in order that his affliction might win life for us. So we have to accept the fact that, if it had not been on our behalf, it would have been impossible for the Son of God to experience suffering.

Barnabas

Recognize God—even in suffering

But it was the Lord's good plan to bruise him . . . , When his soul has been made an offering for sin, then he shall have a multitude of children, many heirs. He shall live again, and God's program shall prosper in his hands.

(ISAIAH 53:10, TLB)

Jesus Christ after his resurrection took his disciples by surprise in his appearances; he presented himself to them under symbols which disguised him; and as soon as he manifested himself, he disappeared. This very same Jesus . . . still takes by surprise souls whose faith is not sufficiently pure and penetrating. . . . There is no moment at which God does not present himself under the guise of some suffering, some consolation, some duty. . . . Could we pierce the veil, and were we vigilant and attentive, God would reveal himself continuously to us and we should rejoice in his action in everything that happened to us. At every occurrence we would say: *Dominus est*—it is the Lord; and in all circumstances we should find a gift from God.

J. P. de Caussade

Don't fear a kind friend

For the Lord is always good. He is always loving and kind, and his faithfulness goes on and on to each succeeding generation.
(PSALM 100:5, TLB)

I expect more goodness from Kate my wife, from Philip Melanchthon, and from others . . . than from my sweet and blessed Savior Jesus Christ; and yet I know for certain that neither she nor any other person on earth will or can suffer that for me which he has suffered. Why then should I be afraid of him? This my foolish weakness grieves me very much. We plainly see in the Gospel how mild and gentle he showed himself toward his disciples; how kindly he passed over their weakness, their presumption, yea, their foolishness. . . . Fie on our unbelieving hearts that we should be afraid of this man who is more loving, friendly, gentle, and compassionate toward us than are our own kindred, our brothers and sisters—yea, than parents toward their own children.

Martin Luther

3.6

The oneness of friendship

*Do two walk together unless
they have agreed to do so?*
(AMOS 3:3)

We speak of being one with a friend, and we mean
that we have a union of purposes and thoughts and
desires. No matter how enthusiastic our friends may
be in their expressions of love and unity, there can
be no real oneness between us unless there are, at
least in some degree, the same likes and dislikes, the
same thoughts and purposes and ideals. Oneness
with Christ means being made a "partaker of his
nature," as well as of his life; for nature and life are,
of course, one.

Hannah Whitall Smith

WE DESIRE HIS PRESENCE

*You have made known to me the path
of life; you will fill me with joy in
your presence, with eternal pleasures
at your right hand.*

(PSALM 16:11)

Let nothing hinder your hearing the Guide's voice

Show me your face, let me hear your voice; for your voice is sweet, and your face is lovely.

(SONG OF SONGS 2:14)

I found I could not live without enjoying the presence of God; and if at any time a dark streak came over me, I could not rest, I could not study, I could not attend to anything with the least satisfaction or benefit, until the medium was again opened between my soul and God.

Charles G. Finney

Though we lose sight of him, he is always there

God has said, "I will never, never fail you nor forsake you." That is why we can say without any doubt or fear, "The Lord is my Helper, and I am not afraid of anything that mere man can do to me."
(HEBREWS 13:5-6, TLB)

Sometimes when his servants forget their purpose, the desires of enjoying God and of leaving this land of exile come before them with tenderness. God is tender indeed considering how little they really serve him. But immediately they return to themselves and reflect how they have him continually before them, and with this they are satisfied. So they offer to his majesty their willingness once more to live for him, the most precious offering that they could make to him. They have no fear of death, but look upon it as a sweet trance. The fact is that he who before gave them those desires with such excessive pain, now gives this sweet desire. So may he be blessed and praised forever!

Teresa of Avila

Don't be distracted again

The LORD appeared to us in the past, saying: "I have loved you with an everlasting love; I have drawn you with loving-kindness. I will build you up again and you will be rebuilt."
(JEREMIAH 31:3-4)

Too late loved I thee, O thou beauty of ancient days, yet ever new! Too late I loved thee! And behold thou were within, and I abroad, there I searched for thee; deformed as I was, running after those beauties which thou hast made. Thou were with me, but I was not with thee. Things held me far from thee—things which, unless they were in thee, were not at all. Thou calledst and shoutedst and didst pierce my deafness. Thou flashedst and shonest and didst dispel my blindness. Thou didst send forth thy fragrance, and I drew in breath and panted for thee. I tasted, and still hunger and thirst. Thou touchedst me, and I burned for thy peace. . . . And now my whole life is nothing but in thine exceeding great mercy. Give what thou commandest, and commend what thou wilt.

Augustine of Hippo

4.3

God knows the way and the future

The LORD will guide you always; he will satisfy your needs in a sun-scorched land and will strengthen your frame. You will be like a well-watered garden, like a spring whose waters never fail.

(ISAIAH 58:11)

Settle this point then, first of all, and let no suggestion of doubt turn you from a steadfast faith in regard to it, that Divine guidance has been promised, and that, if you seek it, you are sure to receive it. Next, you must remember that our God has all knowledge and all wisdom, and that therefore it is very possible he may guide you into paths wherein he knows great blessings are awaiting you, but which, to the short-sighted human eyes around you, seem sure to result in confusion and loss. You must recognize the fact that God's thoughts are not as man's thoughts, nor his ways as man's ways; and that he alone, who knows the end of things from the beginning, can judge of what the results of any course of action may be.

Hannah Whitall Smith

4.4

Draw closer to the Guide each day

I know the plans I have for you, says the Lord.
They are plans for good and not for evil, to give
you a future and a hope. In those days when you
pray, I will listen. You will find me when you
seek me, if you look for me in earnest.
(JEREMIAH 29:11-13, TLB)

To have found God and still to pursue him is the
soul's paradox of love, scorned indeed by the too-
easily-satisfied religionist, but justified in happy experience by the children of the burning heart. St.
Bernard stated this holy paradox in a musical qua-
train that will be instantly understood by every wor-
shipping soul:

> We taste Thee, O Thou Living Bread
>   And long to feast upon Thee still:
> We drink of Thee the Fountainhead
>   And thirst our souls from Thee to fill.

Come near to the holy men and women of the past
and you will soon feel the heat of their desire after
God. . . . And when they found him the finding was
all the sweeter for the long seeking.

A. W. Tozer

4.5

Set your heart on God

I have set the LORD always before me. Because he is at my right hand, I will not be shaken.
(PSALM 16:8)

It is but right that our hearts should be on God, when the heart of God is so much on us. If the Lord of glory can stoop so low as to set his heart on sinful dust, methinks we should easily be persuaded to set our hearts on Christ . . . and ascend to him, in our daily affections. . . . Christian, dost thou not perceive that the heart of God is set upon thee, and that he is still minding thee with tender love? . . . But when he speaks of our regards to him, the case is otherwise: "Can a maid forget her ornaments, or a bride her attire? Yet my people have forgotten me days without number." Let us not give God cause thus to expostulate with us. Rather let our souls get up to God, and visit him every morning, and our hearts be toward him every moment.

Richard Baxter

Seek no other satisfaction

*Whom have I in heaven but you? And I desire
no one on earth as much as you! My health
fails; my spirits droop, yet God remains! He is
the strength of my heart; he is mine forever!*
(PSALM 73:25-26, TLB)

No man is made to be satisfied from himself. . . . We
need to go beyond ourselves, and to fix upon something external to ourselves. We are not independent.
None of us can stand by himself. . . . If a man's life
is to be strong and happy, he must get the foundation of his strength somewhere else than in his own
soul. . . . We are made . . . to need, not things, but
living beings. "My soul thirsteth"—for what? An
abstraction, a possession, riches, a thing? No! "My
soul thirsteth for God, for the living God." Yes,
hearts want hearts. . . . Oh, lay this to heart . . . no
things can satisfy a living soul.

Alexander Maclaren

HE WANTS TO LIVE IN US

*He has kept this secret for centuries
and generations past, but now at last
it has pleased him to tell it to those
who love him and live for him,
and the riches and glory of his plan
are for you. . . . And this is the secret:
that Christ in your hearts
is your only hope of glory.*

(COLOSSIANS 1:26-27, TLB)

Jesus is our example

I have been crucified with Christ: and I myself no longer live, but Christ lives in me. And the real life I now have within this body is a result of my trusting in the Son of God, who loved me and gave himself for me.
(GALATIANS 2:20, TLB)

If you have hitherto known but little of this life of conscience dependence and simple obedience, begin today. Let your Saviour be your example in this. It is his blessed will to live in you, and in you to be again what he was here on earth. He longs only for your acquiescence: he will work it in you. Offer yourself to the Father this day, after the example of the First-begotten, to do nothing of yourself, but only what the Father shows you. Fix your gaze on Jesus as the Example and Promise of what you shall be. Adore him who, for your sake, humbled himself, and showed how blessed the dependent life can be.

Andrew Murray

Reminders of his presence

If the Spirit of him who raised Jesus
from the dead is living in you,
he who raised Christ from the dead
will also give life to your mortal bodies
through his Spirit, who lives in you.
(ROMANS 8:11)

"I am the true Vine." He who speaks is God, in his infinite power able to enter into us. He is man, one with us. He is the crucified one, who won a perfect righteousness and a divine life for us through his death. He is the glorified One, who from the throne gives his Spirit to make his presence real and true. He speaks—oh, listen, not to his words only, but to himself, as he whispers secretly day by day; "I am the true Vine! All that the Vine can ever be to its branch, *I will be to you.*"

Andrew Murray

5.2

Prayer keeps us in touch
with him

And call upon me in the day of trouble: I will deliver thee, and thou shalt glorify me.
(PSALM 50:15, KJV)

If we would be like Jesus we must especially contemplate Jesus praying alone in the wilderness. There is the secret of his wonderful life. What he did and spoke to man was first spoken and lived through with the Father. In communion with him, the anointing with the Holy Spirit was each day renewed. He who would be like him in his walk and conversation must simply begin here, that he follow Jesus into solitude. Even though it cost the sacrifice of night rest, of business, of communion with friends, the time must be found to be alone with the Father. . . . In his secret chamber, with closed door, or in the solitude of the wilderness, God must be found every day. . . . If Christ needed it, how much more we!

Andrew Murray

Leave yourself in his hands

For if these things be in you, and abound,
they make you that ye shall neither be
barren nor unfruitful in the
knowledge of our Lord Jesus Christ.
(2 PETER 1:8, KJV)

"My Father is the Husbandman." This is as blessedly true for us as for Christ. Christ is about to teach his disciples about their being branches. Before he ever uses the word, or speaks at all of abiding in him or bearing fruit, he turns their eyes heavenward to the Father. . . . At the very root of all Christian life lies the thought that God is to do all, that our one work is to give and leave ourselves in his hands, in the confession of utter helplessness and dependence, in the assured confidence that he gives all we need. Christ lived the life of a man exactly as we have to live it. Christ the Vine points to God the Husbandman. As he trusted God, let us trust God, that everything we ought to be and have, as those who belong to the Vine, will be given us from above.

Andrew Murray

5.4

Divine wisdom is available

But the wisdom that comes from heaven is first of all pure; then peace-loving, considerate, submissive, full of mercy and good fruit, impartial and sincere.
(JAMES 3:17)

This divine wisdom is unknown, even to those who pass in the world for persons of extraordinary illumination and knowledge. To whom then is she known, and who can tell us any tidings concerning her? Destruction and death assure us that they have learned with their ears of her fame and renown. It is then, in dying to all things, and in being truly lost to them, passing forward into God, and existing only in him, that we attain to some knowledge of the true wisdom. . . . Scarce do we discover anything thereof, but surprised at the dissimilitude betwixt the truth we thus discover and our former ideas of it, we cry out with St. Paul, "Oh, the depth of the knowledge and wisdom of God! How unsearchable are his judgments, and his ways past finding out."

Jeanne Guyon

5.5

His indwelling reminds us of his love

I won't need to ask the Father to grant you these requests, for the Father himself loves you dearly because you love me and believe that I came from the Father. Yes, I came from the Father into the world and will leave the world and return to the Father.
(JOHN 16:26-28, TLB)

The love of the Father to the Son is not a sentiment—it is a divine life, and infinite energy, an irresistible power. It carried Christ through life and death and the grave. The Father loved him and dwelt in him, and did all for him. So the love of Christ to us too is an infinite living power that will work in us all he delights to give us. The feebleness of our Christian life is that we do not take time to believe that this divine love does really delight in us, and will possess and work all in us. We do not take time to look at the Vine bearing the branch so entirely, working all in it so completely. We strive to do for ourselves what Christ alone can, what Christ . . . longs to do for us.

Andrew Murray

5.6

He awaits an invitation

Look! I have been standing at the door and I
am constantly knocking. If anyone hears me
calling him and opens the door, I will come in
and fellowship with him and he with me.
(REVELATION 3:20, TLB)

Just as our Lord came into human history from the
outside, so he must come into us from the outside.
Have we allowed our personal human lives to become a "Bethlehem" for the Son of God? . . . People
have the idea that because there is good in human
nature (and thank God, there is a lot of good in
human nature), that therefore the Spirit of God is in
every man naturally, meaning that the Spirit of God
in us will become the Christ in us if we let him have
his way. Take that view if you like, but never say it is
the view of the New Testament. It certainly is not
the Lord's view. He said to Nicodemus, "Do not
marvel that I said to you, 'You must be born again.'"

Oswald Chambers

WE SEEK HIM BY FAITH

Cling tightly to your faith in Christ and always keep your conscience clear, doing what you know is right. For some people have disobeyed their consciences and have deliberately done what they knew was wrong. It isn't surprising that soon they lost their faith in Christ after defying God like that.

(1 TIMOTHY 1:19, TLB)

Seeing God with the
eye of faith

*You love him even though you have never
seen him; though not seeing him,
you trust him; and even now you are
happy with the inexpressible joy that
comes from heaven itself.*
(1 PETER 1:8, TLB)

Faith is the least self-regarding of the virtues. It is by its very nature scarcely conscious of its own existence. Like the eye which sees everything in front of it and never sees itself, faith is occupied with the Object upon which it rests and pays no attention to itself at all. While we are looking at God we do not see ourselves—blessed riddance. The man who has struggled to purify himself and has had nothing but repeated failures will experience real relief when he stops tinkering with his soul and looks away to the perfect One. While he looks at Christ the very things he has so long been trying to do will be getting done within him. It will be God working in him to will and to do.

A. W. Tozer

6.1

Faith, the perpetual source

Yet I am standing here depressed and gloomy,
but I will meditate upon your kindness. . . .
Yet day by day the Lord also pours
out his steadfast love upon me,
and through the night I sing his songs
and pray to God who gives me life.
(PSALM 42:6, 8, TLB)

When a severe difficulty or tragedy suddenly comes,
some people may then think about spiritual things.
When the trouble is over, however, they forget their
resolve to seek God. This is like relying on sudden
storms to produce your drinking water. When the
storm is over, the water is gone. How much better
to have water that runs from a perpetual spring! The
new spiritual life in the believer produced by the
Holy Spirit is like a pure spring of water in the mind.

John Owen

Open full access to the source

For in baptism you see how your old,
evil nature died with him and was buried
with him; and then you came up out of death
with him into a new life because you
trusted the Word of the mighty God
who raised Christ from the dead.

(COLOSSIANS 2:12, TLB)

God can do such a work in us by his Spirit, that all that he commands us to do will become about naturally, and not because we feel we *ought to* do it. To make up your mind to praise God may be good, but it is very much better to be so filled with the Holy Spirit that you cannot help praising! What God wants out of us he will first put in. The secret of power for service is to go to Calvary and get rid of the obstacles to the outflow of the Spirit of God, and then ask God for the new life that will bring forth the new fruit. I often hear of things God's children say and do which must grieve him—and it seems hopeless to speak to them about it. The best thing is to ask God to put a *new life* and a *new spirit* in them, so they will not do these things.

Jessie Penn-Lewis

Pay attention to the source of blessing

"If anyone is thirsty, let him come to me and drink. Whoever believes in me, as the Scripture has said, streams of living water will flow from within him." By this he meant the Spirit, whom those who believed in him were later to receive.

(JOHN 7:37-39)

The curse of much modern religion is that it makes us so desperately interested in ourselves, so arrogantly concerned about cleaning ourselves up. Jesus Christ was absolutely interested in God, and the saint is to be a simple, unaffected, natural human being indwelt by the Spirit of God. If the saint is paying attention to the source Jesus Christ, out of him and unconsciously to him are flowing the rivers of living water wherever he goes. Men are either getting better or worse because of us.

Oswald Chambers

Understand prayer and God's love

But let us who live in the light keep sober,
protected by the armor of faith and love.
(1 THESSALONIANS 5:8, TLB)

Perfect prayer and love of God are the same thing. Prayer then is neither a sweet sensation, nor the enchantment of an excited imagination, nor the light of the mind which easily discovers sublime truth in God, nor even a certain comfort in the sight of God. All these things are the exterior gifts, without which love can exist so much the more purely because, being deprived of these things which are only the gifts of God, we will devote ourselves more singly and immediately to himself. This is the love of pure faith.

Fénelon

Give your whole heart to God

Therefore, prepare your minds for action; be self-controlled; set your hope fully on the grace to be given you when Jesus Christ is revealed. As obedient children, do not conform to the evil desires you had when you lived in ignorance. But just as he who called you is holy, so be holy in all you do.
(1 PETER 1:13-15)

We may indeed distinguish three states in which a man may be. He may be yielding his heart more and more to the love of self, in . . . pride, or avarice, or lust, or sloth. Or he may be yielding his heart more and more to the love of God, falteringly, it may be . . . but still really getting to love God more. . . . Or, thirdly, he may . . . by God's grace, have cast out an evil spirit. . . . He may have broken away from the mastery of some bad passion; . . . his will may be poised, as it were, between the one love and the other. Ah! but that can only be for a little while. The balance never lasts; one way or the other the will must incline; one service or the other must be chosen, and that soon.

Francis Paget

6.6

God's love and your response

"Though the mountains be shaken and the hills be removed, yet my unfailing love for you will not be shaken nor my covenant of peace be removed," says the LORD, who has compassion on you.
(ISAIAH 54:10)

Is not he an object of infinite love for whom our Saviour died? Shall not all things in heaven and earth serve him in splendour and glory, for whom the Son of God came down to minister in agonies and suffering? . . . Here consider how you are beloved, and be transported with excess of joy at this wonderful mystery. Leave the trash and vanities of the world, to live here in communion with the blessed Trinity. Imitate St. Paul who counted all things but dross and dung, for the excellency of the knowledge of God in Christ. And thus the works of God serve you in teaching you the knowledge of our Lord and Saviour.

Thomas Traherne

6.7

KNOWING GOD INTIMATELY

My eyes will watch over them for their good, and I will bring them back to this land. I will build them up and not tear them down; I will plant them and not uproot them. I will give them a heart to know me, that I am the LORD. They will be my people, and I will be their God, for they will return to me with all their heart.

(JEREMIAH 24:6-7)

We can know God

"No longer will a man teach his neighbor, or a man his brother, saying, 'Know the LORD,' because they will all know me, from the least of them to the greatest," declares the LORD.

(JEREMIAH 31:34)

Once you have made a decision to know God, you will find that God has placed a desire in your heart to continually draw nearer to him. The closer you grow to God the stronger the desire becomes. It becomes natural, almost habitual, to place God at the center of your life.

Let me assure you that it is only by divine grace that we are able to know God. You must never presume that it is by your own efforts. You are not capable of coming to God unless he has chosen to call you first. "Ye have not chosen me, but I have chosen you" (JOHN 15:16).

Jeanne Guyon

To know God is life eternal

Oh, that we might know the Lord!
Let us press on to know him, and he will
respond to us as surely as the coming
of dawn or the rain of early spring.
(HOSEA 6:3, TLB)

There must therefore some exceeding great thing be always attained in the knowledge of him. To know God is to know goodness. It is to see the beauty of infinite love; to see it attended with almighty power and eternal wisdom; and using both those in the magnifying of its object. It is to see the King of heaven and earth take infinite delight in giving. Whatever knowledge else you have of God it is but superstition. . . . To know him therefore as he is, is to frame the most beautiful idea in all worlds. He delighteth in our happiness more than we: and is of all other the most lovely object. An infinite Lord, who having all riches, honors, and pleasures in his own hand, is infinitely willing to give them unto me.

Thomas Traherne

7.2

Knowing God—much more than knowing *about* God

We have not stopped praying for you and asking God to fill you with the knowledge of his will through all spiritual wisdom and understanding. . . . in order that you may live a life worthy of the Lord and may please him in every way.

(COLOSSIANS 1:9-10)

Do you know God? I am not asking whether you believe things about him; but have you met him? Have you known yourself for certain in his presence? Does he speak to you, and do you know that you speak to him? . . . It matters not where you are as long as you know that this is possible, that Christ died to make it possible. He died "to bring us to God," and to this knowledge. Is your fellowship "with the Father and with his Son Jesus Christ"? O that we might know God! Begin to cry with Job, "Oh, that I knew where I might find him," and you will soon find yourself desiring, hungering to know him. The most vital question to ask about all who claim to be Christian is this: Have they a soul thirst for God?

Martyn Lloyd-Jones

7.3

Satisfaction in knowing God

But we see Jesus, who was made a little lower
than the angels, now crowned with glory and
honor because he suffered death, so that by the
grace of God he might taste death for everyone.
(HEBREWS 2:9)

In human relations we may know a great deal about
a person without at all necessarily coming into any
actual acquaintance with that person; and it is the
same in our relations with God. We may blunder on
for years thinking we know a great deal about him,
but never quite sure of what sort of a Being he
actually is, and consequently never finding any permanent rest or satisfaction. And then, perhaps suddenly, we catch a sight of him as he is revealed in the
face of Jesus Christ . . . and from that moment our
peace flows like a river, and in everything and
through everything, when perhaps we can rejoice in
nothing else, we can rejoice in God. . . . We no
longer need his promises; we have found himself,
and he is enough for every need.

Mrs. Pearsall Smith

God's Presence:
A condition of deliverance

*We know also that the Son of God has come
and has given us understanding, so that we
may know him who is true. And we are in him
who is true—even in his Son Jesus Christ.
He is the true God and eternal life.*
(1 JOHN 5:20)

God, if considered abstracted from the revelation of
himself in the person of Jesus, is a consuming fire;
and if he should look upon us with respect to his
covenant of mercy established in the Mediator, we
could expect nothing from him but indignation and
wrath. But when his Holy Spirit enables us to receive
the record which he has given of his Son, we are
delivered and secured from condemnation; we are
accepted in the Beloved; we are united to him in
whom all the fullness of the Godhead substantially
dwells, and all the riches of divine wisdom, power,
and love are treasured up.

John Newton

Secure in our relationship with God

And without faith it is impossible to please God, because anyone who comes to him must believe that he exists and that he rewards those who earnestly seek him.
(HEBREWS 11:6)

In the case of our human friends we take their existence for granted, not caring whether it is proven or not. Our relationship is such that we could read philosophical arguments designed to prove the non-existence of each other, and perhaps even be convinced by them—and then laugh together over so odd a conclusion. I think that it is something of the same sort of security we should seek in our relationship with God. The more flawless proof of the existence of God is no substitute for it; and if we have that relationship, the most convincing disproof is turned harmlessly aside. If I may say it with reverence, the soul and God laugh together over so odd a conclusion.

Sir Arthur Eddington

Christ's friends share
his secrets

*We know that we have come to know him if we
obey his commands. The man who says,
"I know him," but does not do what he
commands is a liar, and the truth
is not in him.*
(1 JOHN 2:3-4)

The highest proof of true friendship, and one great
source of its blessedness, is the intimacy that holds
nothing back and admits the friend to share our inmost secrets. It is a blessed thing to be Christ's servant;
his redeemed ones delight to call themselves his slaves.
Christ had often spoken of the disciples as his servants.
In his great love our Lord now says: "No longer do I
call you servants." With the coming of the Holy Spirit
a new era was being inaugurated. "The servant
knoweth not what his Lord doeth." He has to obey
without being consulted or admitted into the secret of
all his pastor's plans. "But I have called you friends."
. . . Christ's friends share with him all the secrets the
Father has entrusted to him.

Andrew Murray

7.7

SEEKING GOD ACTIVELY

Listen to me, you who pursue
righteousness and who seek the LORD:
Look to the rock from which you were
cut and to the quarry from which you
were hewn; look to Abraham, your
father, and to Sarah, who gave you
birth. When I called him he was but
one, and I blessed him and made him
many. The LORD will surely comfort
Zion and will look with compassion on
all her ruins; he will make her deserts
like Eden, her wastelands like the
garden of the LORD. Joy and gladness
will be found in her, thanksgiving and
the sound of singing.

(ISAIAH 51:1-3)

8.0

His presence in us

*Do not be afraid . . . for I am with you
and will save you and deliver you.*
(JEREMIAH 42:11)

O my Lord, thou wast in my heart, and demanded
only a simple turning of my mind inward, to make
me perceive thy presence. Oh, Infinite Goodness!
how was I running hither and thither to see thee, my
life was a burden to me, although my happiness was
within myself. I was poor in riches, and ready to
perish with hunger near a table plentifully spread,
and a continual feast. O Beauty, ancient and now;
why have I known thee so late? Alas! I sought thee
where thou wert not, and did not seek thee where
thou wert. It was for want of understanding these
words of thy Gospel, "The kingdom of God cometh
not with observation. . . . The kingdom of God is
within you." This I now experienced. Thou becam-
est my King, and my heart thy kingdom, wherein
thou didst reign supreme, and performed all thy
sacred will.

Jeanne Guyon

God delights in those
who seek him

*Seek the LORD while he may be found; call on
him while he is near. Let the wicked forsake his
way and the evil man his thoughts. Let him
turn to the LORD, and he will have mercy on
him, and to our God, for he will freely pardon.*

(ISAIAH 55:6-7)

What God in his sovereignty may yet do on a world-scale I do not claim to know: but what he will do for the plain man or woman who seeks his face I believe I do know and can tell others. Let any man turn to God in earnest, let him begin to exercise himself unto godliness, let him seek to develop his powers of spiritual receptivity by trust and obedience and humility, and the results will exceed anything he may have hoped in his leaner and weaker days. Any man who by repentance and a sincere return to God will break himself out of the hold in which he has been held, and will go to the Bible itself for his spiritual standards, will be delighted with what he finds there.

A. W. Tozer

To know each other,
we must know him first

How great is the love the Father has lavished on us, that we should be called children of God! And that is what we are! The reason the world does not know us is that it did not know him.

(1 JOHN 3:1)

To get alone—to dare to be alone—with God, this, I am persuaded, is one of the best ways of doing anything in the world. . . . If we are ever to know each other, we must know him first. . . . I believe that we do most for those whom God has begun to teach us to love, not by constantly thinking of their goodness, their grace, their simplicity, but by never thinking of them apart from God, by always connecting their beauty and purity with a higher Beauty and a higher Purity, by seeing God in them. Let us learn to make every thought of admiration and love a kind of prayer of intercession and thanksgiving. Thus human love will correct itself with, and find its root in, divine love. But this we can do only if we are willing to be alone with him.

Forbes Robinson

8.3

When we seek the truth, we find him

I love those who love me,
and those who seek me find me.
(PROVERBS 8:17)

Remember that when with thine understanding thou goest forth to find God, in order to rest in him, thou must place neither limit nor comparison with thy weak and narrow imaginations. For he is infinite beyond all comparison; he is through all and in all, and in him are all things. Himself thou wilt find within thy soul, whenever thou shalt seek him in truth, that is, in order to find thyself. For his delight is to be with us, the children of men, to make us worthy of him, thou he hath no need of us. In meditation do not be so tied down to certain points that thou wilt meditate on them alone; but wherever thou shalt find rest, there stop and taste the Lord, at whatever step he shall will to communicate himself to thee.

Lorenzo Scupoli

Sinners fly rapidly into their Savior's arms

"In those days, at that time," declares the LORD, "the people of Israel and the people of Judah together will go in tears to seek the LORD their God. They will ask the way to Zion and turn their faces toward it. They will come and bind themselves to the LORD in an everlasting covenant that will not be forgotten."

(JEREMIAH 50:4-5)

The self-righteous, relying on the many good works he imagines he has performed, seems to hold salvation in his own hand, and considers heaven as a just reward of his merits. In the bitterness of his zeal he exclaims against all sinners, and represents the gates of mercy as barred against them, and heaven as a place to which they have no claim. What need have such self-righteous persons of a Saviour? They are already burdened with the load of their own merits. Oh, how long they bear the flattering load, while sinners divested of everything, fly rapidly on the wings of faith and love into their Saviour's arms, who freely bestows on them that which he has so freely promised!

Jeanne Guyon

8.5

Partaker of his happiness
and his eternity

Where can I go from your Spirit? Where can I flee from your presence? . . . If I rise on the wings of the dawn, if I settle on the far side of the sea, even there your hand will guide me, your right hand will hold me fast.
(PSALM 139:7-10)

O immeasurable goodness of our Creator! O inestimable mercy! Himself in nothing ever needing man, yet of his goodness alone he created man; creating, he adorned him with reason, that he might be able to be partaker of his happiness and his eternity, and so with him possess forever joy and gladness. Still further, while man in many things is contrary to him, knowingly and willfully doeth many things although they are displeasing to him, yet he warneth him to return, to seek again the mercy of his Creator, nor for any sin, however grievous, presume to despair. For he is the fountain of loving-kindness and mercy, and all, with whatever stain of sin they are defiled, he longeth to cleanse; cleansed, to give them the joy of everlasting life.

Anselm

8.6

Surrender yourself
wholly to him

But if from there you seek the LORD your God,
you will find him if you look for him with all
your heart and with all your soul.
(DEUTERONOMY 4:29)

Do you, then, now at this moment, surrender yourself wholly to him? You answer, Yes. Then, my dear
friend, begin at once to reckon that you are his, that
he has taken you, and that he is working in you to
will and to do of his good pleasure, and keep on
reckoning this. You will find it a great help to put
your reckoning into words, and say over and over to
yourself and to your God, "Lord, I am thine; I do
yield myself up entirely to thee, and I believe that
thou dost take me. I leave myself with thee. Work in
me all the good pleasure of thy will, and I will only
lie still in thy hands and trust thee."

Hannah Whitall Smith

UNDERSTANDING GOD

*I pray . . . that Christ may dwell in
your hearts through faith.
And I pray that you, being rooted and
established in love, may have power,
together with all the saints, to grasp
how wide and long and high and deep
is the love of Christ, and to know this
love that surpasses knowledge—
that you may be filled to the measure
of all the fullness of God.*

(EPHESIANS 3:16-19)

Trust God's wisdom

*He made known to us the mystery of
his will according to his good pleasure,
which he purposed in Christ.*
(EPHESIANS 1:9)

I can hardly recollect a single plan of mine, of which
I have not since seen reason to be satisfied that, had
it taken place in season and circumstances just as I
proposed, it would, humanly speaking, have proved
my ruin; or at least it would have deprived me of the
greater good the Lord had designed for me. We
judge things by their present appearance, but the
Lord sees them in their consequences; if we could do
so likewise, we should be perfectly of his mind; but
as we cannot, it is an unspeakable mercy that he will
manage for us, whether we are pleased with his
management or not; and it is spoken of one of his
heaviest judgments, when he gives any person or
people up to the way of their own hearts, and to talk
after their own counsels.

John Newton

The unseen Lord a "living bright reality"

I will praise the LORD, who counsels me;
even at night my heart instructs me.
(PSALM 16:7)

How few there are to whom the unseen Lord is a "living bright reality." The result is that there is little personal devotion to him, and still less knowledge of his voice, and his personal individual control of the believer's life. So much knowledge about the Lord Jesus with so little direct and personal communication with him over every detail of life! So little close walking and talking with him, but so much running about and questioning of each other over the simplest matters, made plain to the Word of God—and to be made plain again to each obedient heart seeking the face of the Living Lord!

Jessie Penn-Lewis

God's wisdom is ours

Then you will understand the fear of the LORD
and find the knowledge of God. For the LORD
gives wisdom, and from his mouth come
knowledge and understanding. He holds
victory in store for the upright, he is a shield
to those whose walk is blameless.
(PROVERBS 2:5-7)

It is a mistake to see a sign from heaven; to run from counselor to counselor; to cast a lot; or to trust to some chance coincidence. Not that God may not reveal his will thus; but because it is hardly the behavior of a child with its Father. There is a more excellent way. Let the heart be quieted and still in the presence of God. . . . Let the voice of the Son of God hush into perfect rest the storms that sweep the lake of the inner life, and ruffle its calm surface. . . . Remembering that all who lack wisdom are to ask it of God . . . let us quietly appropriate him, in that capacity, by faith; and then go forward, perhaps not conscious of any increase of wisdom . . . but sure that we shall be guided as each new step must be taken, or word spoken, or decision made.

F. B. Meyer

9.3

Crave the knowledge of God

Many peoples will come and say, "Come, let us go up to the mountain of the LORD, to the house of the God of Jacob. He will teach us his ways, so that we may walk in his paths." The law will go out from Zion, the word of the LORD from Jerusalem.

(ISAIAH 2:3)

Beware the common habit of putting confidence in books, as such. It takes a determined effort of the mind to break free from the error of making books and teachers ends in themselves. . . . The function of a good book is to stand like a signpost directing the reader toward the Truth and Life. That book serves best which early makes itself unnecessary, just as a signpost serves best after it is forgotten, after the traveler has arrived safely at his desired haven. The work of a good book is to incite the reader to moral action, to turn his eyes toward God and urge him forward. . . . [One] cannot love a God who is no more than a deduction from a text. He will crave to know God with a vital awareness that goes beyond words, and to live in the intimacy of personal communion.

A. W. Tozer

9.4

Learn to hear God's voice

The LORD came and stood there,
calling as at the other times,
"Samuel! Samuel!" Then Samuel said,
"Speak, for your servant is listening."
(1 SAMUEL 3:10)

How rare it is that the soul is sufficiently stilled to let God speak! The least murmur of our foolish wishes, the least murmur of self-interest, confuses the message of the Spirit of God. We hear him speaking and asking for something, but we have no idea what he is saying, and often we are as glad not to guess. The least reservation, the least consideration of self, the least fear of hearing too clearly that God is asking for more than we want to give him—any of these will disturb the Word within. Need we then wonder that so many people, even pious people, but still pleasure loving, full of foolish desires, of false wisdom, of complacency, cannot hear; and consider this inner Word the imagination of fanatics?

Fénelon

Access to God a high
honor and privilege

*Evil men do not understand justice, but those
who seek the LORD understand it fully.*
(PROVERBS 28:5)

The secret of the Lord is with them that fear him.
He deals familiarly with them. He calls them not
servants only, but friends; and he treats them as
friends. He affords them more than promises, for he
opens to them the plan of his great designs from
everlasting to everlasting, shows them the strong
foundations and inviolable securities of his favor
towards them, the height, and depth, and length,
and breadth of his love, which passeth knowledge,
and the unsearchable riches of his grace. . . . The
men of the world would account it a high honor and
privilege to have an unrestrained liberty of access to
an earthly king; but what words can express the
privilege and honor of believers, who whenever they
please, have audience with the King of kings.

John Newton

Indescribable seasons with God

The LORD your God is with you, he is mighty
to save. He will take great delight in you,
he will quiet you with his love,
he will rejoice over you with singing.

(ZEPHANIAH 3:17)

I used to have, when I was a young Christian, many seasons of communing with God which cannot be described in words. And not unfrequently these seasons would end in an impression on my mind like this: "Go see that thou tell no man." I did not understand this at the time and several times I . . . tried to tell my Christian brethren what communications the Lord had made to me. . . . But I soon found that it would not do to tell what was passing between the Lord and my soul. They could not understand it. They would look surprised, and sometimes, I thought, incredulous; and I soon learned to . . . say but little about them.

Charles G. Finney

Week Ten

GOD'S WORK IN US

For we are God's workmanship, created in Christ Jesus to do good works, which God prepared in advance for us to do.

(EPHESIANS 2:10)

10.0

Salvation: "The life of God in the soul of man"

Therefore, my dear friends, as you have always obeyed—not only in my presence, but now much more in my absence—continue to work out your salvation with fear and trembling.

(PHILIPPIANS 2:12)

The old Puritan writer who defined salvation as "the life of God in the soul of man" was entirely right. Only do not fail to bear in mind that the man in whom he dwells is not himself passive. . . . Indolent activity, even in the name of orthodox belief, can never hold fellowship with essential energy—which is what God is. Yes, there are hands unseen working with our hands. There is a will omnipotent energizing our wills. There is a wisdom ineffable informing our minds. . . . There is a strength untold directing our members. There is a divine craftsman repeating himself in us. And all in such a manner that our individuality is not thereby destroyed but developed. We are ourselves workers together with him, pledged to do our part, though always aware that without him we are nothing.

J. Stuart Holden

10.1

The joy of our deliverance from sin

For the power of the life-giving Spirit—
and this power is mine through Christ Jesus—
has freed me from the vicious circle
of sin and death.
(ROMANS 8:2, TLB)

It is only so long as we are standing in the joy of our Lord, in the joy of our deliverance from sin, in the joy of his love, and what he is for us, in the joy of his presence, that we have the power to serve and obey. It is only when made free from every master, from sin and self and the law, and only when rejoicing in this liberty, that we have the power to render service that is satisfying either to God or to ourselves. "I will see you again," Jesus said, "and your heart shall rejoice, and your joy shall no man take from you" (John 16:22). Joy is the evidence and the condition of the abiding personal presence of Jesus.

Andrew Murray

10.2

Indwelt by the Spirit

But this precious treasure—this light and power that now shine within us—is held in a perishable container, that is, in our weak bodies. Everyone can see that the glorious power within must be from God and is not our own.

(2 Corinthians 4:7, TLB)

God's "illuminating vessels" are not always outwardly beautiful ones! Man thinks so much of outward appearance; of a noble presence; of fluency of speech; of strength of body; but God chooses to do his mightiest work with instruments that are often manifestly weak, base, and despised. Moreover he allows them also to remain "contemptible" in the eyes of others, lest they glory in the instrument, and fail to see the power of God.

Jessie Penn-Lewis

Energized to witness

*I pray that out of his glorious riches he may
strengthen you with power through
his Spirit in your inner being.*
(EPHESIANS 3:16)

This is just what is needed today—believers indwelt by
the Holy Spirit, revealing their resurrection union with
the Risen Ascended Lord, so filled with the written
Word that the Eternal Spirit of the Father can come
upon them and energize them to witness with boldness, so that they wield the "sword of the Spirit" with
such effect that men will be pricked to the heart by the
two-edged Word. . . . A Pentecost which will produce
such witnesses the Church and the world surely need.
[They need] believers who will not preach their own
ideas, or even their experiences, as a testimony, but the
Word of God in the message of Calvary and the
Resurrection and Ascension of the coming Lord, with
such power of God upon them that these stupendous
facts become facts to all who hear, and a mighty energy
in their lives.

Jessie Penn-Lewis

10.4

God's purpose for us

But the Counselor, the Holy Spirit,
whom the Father will send in my name,
will teach you all things and will remind
you of everything I have said to you.
(JOHN 14:26)

"What does God do all day?" once asked a little boy. . . . Unfortunately most of us are not even boys in religious intelligence, but only very unthinking babes. It no more occurs to us that God is engaged in any particular work in the world than it occurs to a little child that its father does anything except be a father. . . . The first great epoch in a Christian's life, after the awe and wonder of its dawn, is when there breaks into his mind some sense that Christ has a purpose for mankind, a purpose beyond him and his needs . . . a purpose which embraces every kindred and nation formed, which regards not their spiritual good alone, but the welfare in every part, their progress, their health, their work, their wages, their happiness in this present world.

Henry Drummond

One in heaven ever lives to intercede

My little children, I am telling you this so that you will stay away from sin. But if you sin, there is someone to plead for you before the Father. His name is Jesus Christ, the one who is all that is good and who pleases God completely.

(1 JOHN 2:1, TLB)

What a comfort and what hope there is to fill our breasts when we think of one in heaven who ever lives to intercede for us, because "his compassion fails not!" . . . The compassion of our Lord well fits him for being the great high priest of Adam's fallen, lost and helpless race. And if he is filled with such compassion that it moves him at the Father's right hand to intercede for us, then by every token we should have the same compassion on . . . those exposed to divine wrath, as would move us to pray for them. Just insofar as we are compassionate will we be prayerful for others. Compassion does not expend its force simply saying, "Be ye warmed; be ye clothed," but drives us to our knees in prayer for those who need Christ and his grace.

E. M. Bounds

10.6

Christic in heaven revealed in us

We are hard pressed on every side, but not crushed; perplexed, but not in despair; persecuted, but not abandoned; struck down, but not destroyed. We always carry around in our body the death of Jesus, so that the life of Jesus may also be revealed in our body.

(2 CORINTIANS 4:8-10)

It is very striking to find, in going through the chapters in the Acts, that all the early believers talked about *Christ risen and ascended to the throne in heaven,* but very little is said about personal *inward* experience. There is hardly a trace of it. They did not preach what they had obtained inwardly, but proclaimed a glorified Christ on the throne. This shows that a true baptism of the Holy Spirit does not turn the recipient *inward* to himself, to cultivate some personal experience and have a good time, but turns him God-ward and man-ward. The Christ they talked about was a *Christ in heaven.* Peter said, "He being by the right hand of God exalted, hath poured forth this. . . ."

Jessie Penn-Lewis

IDENTIFICATION WITH HIM

*As a result, he does not live the rest of
his earthly life for evil human desires,
but rather for the will of God.*

(1 PETER 4:2)

Choosing to identify
with Christ

For to be sure, he was crucified in weakness,
yet he lives by God's power. Likewise,
we are weak in him, yet by God's power
we will live with him to serve you.
(2 CORINTHIANS 13:4)

Many of us are not living in the domain in which Christianity alone can be lived—the domain of deliberate identification with Jesus Christ. It takes time, and it ought to take time, and the time is not misspent for the soul who will wait before God and accept his appointment for his individual life.

Oswald Chambers

All that God wants us to be

And he died for all, that those who live should no longer live for themselves but for him who died for them and was raised again.
(2 CORINTHIANS 5:15)

Jesus Christ revealed what a normal man should be and in so doing showed how we may become all that God wants us to be. When we are sanctified we do not get something like a landslide of holiness from heaven; we are introduced into a relationship of oneness with God, and as our Lord met antagonistic forces and overcame them, so must we. The life Jesus lived is a type of our life after sanctification. We are apt to make sanctification the end; it is only the beginning. Our holiness as saints consists in the exclusive dedication to God of our powers.

Oswald Chambers

Reinstating humanity into communion with God

Now if we are children, then we are heirs—heirs of God and co-heirs with Christ, if indeed we share in his sufferings in order that we may also share in his glory.
(ROMANS 8:17)

Never separate the incarnation and the atonement. The incarnation was not for the self-realization of God, but for the purpose of removing sin and reinstating humanity into communion with God. Jesus Christ became incarnate for one purpose: to make a way back to God, that man might stand before him as he was created to do, the friend and lover of God himself. The atonement means infinitely more than we can conceive; it means that we can be morally identified with Jesus Christ until we understand what the apostle Paul meant when he said, "It is no longer I who live, but Christ lives in me."

Oswald Chambers

11.3

Life from him by
deliberate appointment

I want to know Christ and the power of his resurrection and the fellowship of sharing in his sufferings, becoming like him in his death.
(PHILIPPIANS 3:10)

How many of us have dispassionately and clearly looked at Philippians 3:10? Paul is not speaking poetically but expressing plain, blunt, simple, spiritual, heroic fact. "That I may know him" (not what he can do, not what I can proclaim that he has done for me), "and the power of his resurrection" (that I continually receive my life from him by deliberate appointment on my own part), "and the fellowship of his sufferings" (that I enter determinedly into his relationship with things, which means going contrary to my natural intuitions); "being conformable to his death."

Oswald Chambers

Exclusive allegiance to God

*My conscience is clear, but that does not make
me innocent. It is the Lord who judges me.*
(1 CORINTHIANS 4:4)

Here and there people flee from public altercation
into the sanctuary of private *virtuousness*. But anyone who does this must shut his mouth and eyes to
the injustice around him. Only at the cost of self-de-
ception can he keep himself pure from the contami-
nation arising from responsible action. In spite of all
that he does, what he leaves undone will rob him of
his peace of mind. He will either go to pieces because of this disquiet, or become the most hypocritical of Pharisees. Who stands fast? Only the man
whose final standard is not his reason, his principles,
his conscience, his freedom, or his virtue, but who is
ready to sacrifice all this when he is called to obedient and responsible action in faith and in exclusive
allegiance to God.

Dietrich Bonhoeffer

The life behind the action

He died for us so that, whether we are awake or asleep, we may live together with him.
(1 THESSALONIANS 5:10)

There is a whole universe of moral and psychological difference between saying, "Christ is my pattern, and if I try I can be like him," and saying "I am so far from goodness that Christ had to die for me that I might be forgiven." The one is still in the world of legalism, and its center of attention is still the self. The other is in the world of grace, and its center of attention is another to whose love it is our whole and only aim to give ourselves. The one must always lack what the other increasingly has, the spontaneity and wholeheartedness that come when there is the whole force of an emotionally integrated life behind action.

Lesslie Newbigin

Manifest the life of
the Son of God

Whoever claims to live in him
must walk as Jesus did.
(1 JOHN 2:6)

We have to form habits to express what God's grace
has done in us. It is not a question of being saved
from hell, but of being saved in order to manifest the
life of the Son of God in our mortal flesh, and it is
the disagreeable things which make us exhibit
whether or not we are manifesting his life. Do I
manifest the essential sweetness of the Son of God,
or the essential irritation of myself apart from him?
The only thing that will enable me to enjoy the
disagreeable is the keen enthusiasm of letting the life
of the Son of God manifest itself in me. No matter
how disagreeable a thing may be, say, "Lord, I am
delighted to obey Thee in this matter," and instantly
the Son of God will press to the front, and there will
be manifested in my human life that which glorifies
Jesus.

Oswald Chambers

11.7

Scripture: The Focal Point of Meditation

*Do not let this Book of the Law depart
from your mouth; meditate on it day
and night, so that you may be careful
to do everything written in it. Then
you will be prosperous and successful.*

(JOSHUA 1:8)

12.0

Retreat: a time of withdrawal and recollection

But Jesus often withdrew to
lonely places and prayed.
(LUKE 5:16)

Take, according to when we are free and feel the need, certain days entirely for withdrawal and recollection. It is thus that at the feet of Jesus Christ we heal secretly all the wounds of our hearts, we wipe off all the bad imprints of the world. This even helps our health because, if a person knows how to make simple use of these short retreats, they rest the body no less than the spirit.

Fénelon

Focus on God's presence

Even though I walk through the valley of the
shadow of death, I will fear no evil,
for you are with me; your rod
and your staff, they comfort me.
(PSALM 23:4)

When you come to God in prayer, open your Bible
to where you have been meditating. Remember at
this point that your main objective is to focus on
God's presence. Your Scripture verse will keep your
mind from straying to other things.

This method of praying can be used by those of
you with even a small portion of faith, because it will
keep your mind from distractions. This way even a
small amount of faith will enlarge in proportion
when viewed by itself.

Oh, dear one, God has promised that he would
come and make his abode with him who does his
will. He has promised to dwell in our innermost
being—the new Holy of Holies place.

Jeanne Guyon

12.2

Meditation: The heart appropriates the Word

But his delight is in the law of the LORD,
and on his law he meditates day and night.
(PSALM 1:2)

It is in meditation that the heart holds and appropriates the Word. Just as in reflection the understanding grasps all the meaning and bearings of a truth, so in meditation the heart assimilates it and makes it a part of its own life. We need continual reminding that the heart means the will and affection. The meditation of the heart implies desire, acceptance, surrender, love. Out of the heart are the issues of life; what the heart truly believes, that it receives with love and joy, and allows to master and rule the life. The intellect gathers and prepares the food on which we are to feed. In meditation the heart takes it in and feeds on it.

Andrew Murray

Find Jesus Christ in solitude
and in silence

*I have set the LORD always before me. Because
he is at my right hand, I will not be shaken.*
(PSALM 16:8)

How can we find Jesus Christ if we do not seek him
in the conditions of his mortal life, that is to say, in
solitude, in silence, in poverty and suffering? . . .
The saints find him in heaven, in the splendor of
glory and in ineffable joy, but it is after having lived
with him on earth in shame, suffering and humiliation. To be Christians is to be imitators of Jesus
Christ. In what can we imitate him except in his
humiliations? Nothing else can draw us to him. As
all-powerful, we ought to adore him; as just, we
ought to fear him; as good and merciful, we ought
to love him with all our strength; as humble, submissive, lowly, and faithful unto death, we ought to
imitate him.

Fénelon

12.4

Withdraw from men
to enjoy the Lord

*On my bed I remember you; I think of you
through the watches of the night.*
(PSALM 63:6)

Concerning the fittest place for heavenly meditation
it is sufficient to say that the most convenient is
some private retirement. . . . Withdraw thyself from
all society, even the society of godly men, that thou
mayest awhile enjoy the society of the Lord. . . .
Christ had his accustomed place, and consequently
accustomed duty, and so much we. . . . Only there is
a wide difference in the object: Christ meditates on
the sufferings that our sins had deserved, so that the
wrath of his Father passed through all his soul; but
we are to meditate on the glory he hath purchased,
that the love of the Father, and the joy of the Spirit,
may enter at our thoughts, revive our affections, and
overflow our souls.

Richard Baxter

Time alone with yourself

The LORD would speak to Moses face to face, as a man speaks with his friend.
(EXODUS 33:11)

If you take my advice you will try to get a certain amount of time alone with yourself. . . . Sometimes when we are with others . . . we persuade ourselves that we believe more than we do. . . . We grow enthusiastic, we speak of religious emotions and experiences. This is, perhaps, sometimes good. But when we are alone we see just how much we really believe. . . . We go face to face with him, and our heat and passion go, and what is really permanent remains. We begin to recognize how very little love we have, how very little pleasure in that which is alone of lasting importance. Then we see how poor and hollow and unloving we are; then, I think, we also begin to see that this poverty, this hollowness, this unloving void, can be filled only by him who fills all in all.

Forbes Robinson

12.6

Seek him who sought us

As the deer pants for streams of water,
so my soul pants for you, O God.
My soul thirsts for God, for the living God.
When can I go and meet with God?
(PSALM 42:1-2)

Behold, Father, behold, and see and approve; and be it pleasing in the sight of your mercy, that I may find grace before you, that the inward parts of your words be opened to my knocking. I beseech by our Lord Jesus Christ thy Son, the Man of your right hand, the Son of man . . . through whom you sought us, not seeking you, but sought us, that we might seek you—your Word, through whom you made all things and among them, me also—your only-begotten, through Whom you called to adoption the believing people, and therein me also—I beseech you by him, who sits at your right hand and intercedes with you for us, in whom are hidden all the treasures of wisdom and knowledge. These do I seek in your books.

Augustine of Hippo

12.7

Desire to Be Intimate with God

*I keep asking that the God of our Lord
Jesus Christ, the glorious Father,
may give you the Spirit of wisdom
and revelation, so that you
may know him better.*

(Ephesians 1:17)

Dryness, even in the
way of *meditation*

He turned rivers into a desert,
flowing springs into thirsty ground.
(PSALM 107:33)

There is great dryness even in the way of *meditation;* the bread of prayer is often without taste; the most beautiful thoughts often leave nothing affective in the soul, and sometimes the drynesses pass into powerlessness to meditate. But the soul . . . does not leave its meditation; it strains itself, it goes over and over its material for meditation, and when it can no longer do anything it resolves to suffer without inquietude, this cross being of greater merit than affections or thoughts. . . . When the contemplative dryness continues to battle with the senses, it suffers wearisome dryness till it has thoroughly stripped itself. . . . The soul will no longer have anything, and it will not desire anything, but the good pleasure of God.

François Malaval

13.1

Holy desire helped by devout contemplation

My soul yearns, even faints,
for the courts of the LORD; my heart
and my flesh cry out for the living God.
(PSALM 84:2)

Holy desire is much helped by devout contemplation. Meditation on our spiritual need, and on God's readiness and ability to correct it, aids desire to grow. Serious thought engaged in before praying increases desire, makes it more insistent, and tends to save us from the menace of private prayer—wandering thought. We fail much more in desire than in its outward expression. We retain the form, while the inner life fades and almost dies. One might well ask whether the feebleness of our desires for God . . . is not the cause of our so little praying. . . . Do we really feel these inward pantings of desire after heavenly treasures? Do the inbred groanings of desire stir our souls to mighty wrestlings? Also for us! The fire burns altogether too low.

E. M. Bounds

13.2

The sweetness of communion with God

I will sing to the LORD all my life;
I will sing praise to my God as long as I live.
May my meditation be pleasing to him,
as I rejoice in the LORD.
(PSALM 104:33-34)

What is more easy and sweet than meditation? Yet in this hath God commended his love, that by meditation it is enjoyed. As nothing is more easy than to think, so nothing is more difficult than to think well. The easiness of thinking we received from God, the difficulty of thinking well proceeded from ourselves. Yet in truth, it is far more easy to think well than ill, because good thoughts be sweet and delightful. Evil thoughts are full of discontent and trouble. So that an evil habit and custom have made it difficult to think well, not Nature. For by nature nothing is so difficult as to think amiss.

Thomas Traherne

Time for recollection

Check up on yourselves. Are you really Christians? Do you pass the test? Do you feel Christ's presence and power more and more within you? Or are you just pretending to be Christians when actually you are not at all?

(2 CORINTHIANS 13:5, TLB)

Take some time for recollection, and ask your own conscience, seriously, how matters stand between the blessed God and your soul? Whether they are as they once were, and as you could wish them to be, if you saw your life just drawing to a period, and were to pass immediately into the eternal state? Once serious thought of eternity shames a thousand vain excuses, with which, in the forgetfulness of it, we are ready to delude our own souls. And when you feel that secret misgiving of heart, which will naturally arise on this occasion, do not endeavor to palliate the matter, and to find out slight and artful coverings for what you cannot forbear secretly condemning, but honestly fall under the conviction, and be humbled for it.

Philip Doddridge

13.4

Creative silence issues
out in might

*In repentance and rest is your salvation,
in quietness and trust is your strength.*
(ISAIAH 30:15)

All beneficent and creative power gathers itself together in silence, ere it issues out in might. . . .
Silence came before creation, and the heavens were spread without a word. Christ was born at dead of night; and though there has been no power like him, "He did not strive nor cry, neither was his voice heard in the streets." Nowhere can you find any beautiful work, any noble design, any durable endeavor, that was not matured in long and patient silence ere it spake out in its accomplishment. . . .
There it is that the soul, enlarging all its dimensions at once, acquires a greater and more vigorous being, and gathers up its collective forces to bear down upon the piecemeal difficulties of life and scatter them to dust.

James Martineau

13.5

Biblical spiritual meditation

How sweet are your words to my taste,
sweeter than honey to my mouth!
(PSALM 119:103)

Real communion does exist between Christ and believers. That happens when believers practice spiritual meditation in a biblical way. Those who sow such seeds will reap a harvest! Such thoughts about Christ are most acceptable to him. Such thoughts best prepare believers to receive Christ's teaching. Failure to meditate will certainly cause believers to lose their joy in Christ. Sometimes they are too busy; sometimes they are careless; sometimes they are spiritually cold. These are not ways to have their spiritual joy abound. We should think about Christ's glory in heaven now.

John Owen

Our goal is union with him

What is more, I consider everything a loss compared to the surpassing greatness of knowing Christ Jesus my Lord, for whose sake I have lost all things. I consider them rubbish, that I may gain Christ.
(PHILIPPIANS 3:8)

In order to see him as, one day, it will be possible to see and cling to him, we cleanse ourselves from every stain of sin and evil desire, sanctifying ourselves by his name. For he is the source of our happiness and the very end of all our aspirations. We elect him, whom, by neglect, we lost. We offer him our allegiance—for "allegiance" and "religion" are at root, the same. We pursue him with our love so that when we reach him we may rest in perfect happiness in him who is our goal. For our goal . . . is nothing else than union with him whose spiritual embrace, if I may so speak, can alone fecundate the intellectual soul and fill it with true virtue.

Augustine of Hippo

13.7

GOD'S SURE WORD ON HOW TO LIVE

And we also thank God continually because, when you received the word of God, which you heard from us, you accepted it not as the word of men, but as it actually is, the word of God, which is at work in you who believe.

(1 THESSALONIANS 2:13)

14.0

In the Word of God
the divine life appears

Do not snatch the word of truth from my
mouth, for I have put my hope in your laws.
I will always obey your law, for ever and ever.
I will walk about in freedom,
for I have sought out your precepts.
I will speak of your statutes before kings.
(PSALM 119:43-46)

True life is found only in God. But that life cannot
be imparted to us unless set before us in some shape
in which we know and apprehend it. It is in the Word
of God that the Invisible Divine life takes shape, and
brings itself within our reach, and becomes commu-
nicable. The life, the thoughts, the sentiments, the
power of God are embodied in his words. And it is
only through his Word that the life of God can really
enter into us. His Word is the seed of the heavenly
life.

Andrew Murray

True doctrine should be certain and unquestioned

Now I commit you to God and to the word of his grace, which can build you up and give you an inheritance among all those who are sanctified.

(ACTS 20:32)

Not all the articles of true doctrine are of the same sort. Some are so necessary to know that they should be certain and unquestioned by all men as the proper principles of religion. Such are: God is one; Christ is God and the Son of God; our salvation rests in God's mercy; and the like. Among the churches there are other articles of doctrine disputed which still do not break the unity of faith. . . . Here are the apostle's words: "Let us therefore, as many as are perfect, be of the same mind; and if you be differently minded in anything, God shall reveal this also to you." Does this not sufficiently indicate that a difference of opinion over these nonessential matters should in no wise be the basis of schism among Christians?

John Calvin

14.2

Stirred in the inner life
by the Word

*I am not ashamed of the gospel, because it is
the power of God for the salvation of everyone
who believes: first for the Jew,
then for the Gentile.*
(ROMANS 1:16)

The true aim of education, study, reading, is to be
found, not in what is brought into us, but in what is
brought out of ourselves by the awakening into
active exercise of our inward power. This is as true
of the study of the Bible as of any other study. God's
Word works its true blessing only when the truth it
brings to us has stirred the inner life, and reproduced
itself in resolve, trust, love or adoration. When the
heart has received the Word through the mind, and
has had its spiritual powers called out and exercised
on it, the Word is no longer void, but has done that
whereunto God has sent. It has become part of our
life, and strengthened us for new purpose and effort.

Andrew Murray

14.3

The gospel—a solace and comfort

The unfolding of your words gives light;
it gives understanding to the simple.
(PSALM 119:130)

The gospel is like a fresh, mild, and cool air in the extreme heat of summer, a solace and comfort in the anguish of the conscience. But as this heat proceeds from the rays of the sun, so likewise the terrifying of the conscience must proceed from the preaching of the law, to the end that we may know we have offended against the laws of God. Now, when the mind is refreshed and quickened again by the cool air of the gospel, we must not then be idle, or lie down and sleep. That is, when our consciences are settled in peace, quieted and comforted through God's spirit, we must prove our faith by such good works as God has commanded.

Martin Luther

To reach full spiritual maturity

. . . until we all reach unity in the faith
and in the knowledge of the Son of God
and become mature, attaining to the whole
measure of the fullness of Christ.
(EPHESIANS 4:13)

Indeed, it is better to keep quiet and be, than to make fluent professions and not be. No doubt it is a fine thing to instruct others, but only if the speaker practices what he preaches. . . . A man who has truly mastered the utterances of Jesus will also be able to apprehend his silence, and thus reach full spiritual maturity, so that his own words have the force of factions and his silences the significance of speech. Nothing is hidden from the Lord; even our most secret thoughts are ever present to him. Whatever we do, then, let it be done as though he himself were dwelling within us, we being as it were his temples and he within us as their God. For in fact, that is literally the case; and in proportion as we rightly love him, so it will become clear to our eyes.

Ignatius of Antioch

14.5

Yes, you may rise

If we claim to be without sin,
we deceive ourselves and the truth is not in us.
If we confess our sins, he is faithful and just
and will forgive us our sins and
purify us from all unrighteousness.
(1 JOHN 1:8-9)

The great tempter of men has two devices with which he plies us at two different stages. Before we have fallen, he tells us that one fall does not matter: it is a trifle; why should we not know the taste of the forbidden fruit? We can easily recover ourselves again. After we have fallen, on the contrary, he tells us that it is hopeless: we are given over to sin, and need not attempt to rise. Both are false. It is a terrible falsehood to say that to fall does not matter. Even by one fall there is something lost that can never be recovered. . . . To those who feel themselves fallen I come, in Christ's name, to say, Yes, you may rise. If we could ascend to heaven today and scan the ranks of the blessed, should we not find multitudes among them who were once sunk low as man can fall?

James Stalker

14.6

Listen to Jesus

This is the Father's will that we should listen to what
the man Jesus says and give ear to his Word. You are
not to try to be clever in connection with his Word,
to master it or to argue about it, but simply to hear
it. Then the Holy Spirit will come and dispose your
heart so that you will believe and say from the
bottom of your heart concerning the preaching of
the divine Word: "That is God's Word and is the
pure truth" and you will risk your life upon it. But if
you yourself want to be heard, and to obliterate the
Word of Christ with your own reason, if you attempt
to subject the Word to your own ideas . . . if you
ponder it as though you were in doubt about it,
wanting to judge it according to your own mind,
that is not listening to it, or being a disciple.

Martin Luther

ESTABLISHED IN THE WORD OF GOD

*I write to you, fathers, because you
have known him who is from the
beginning. I write to you, young men,
because you are strong, and the word of
God lives in you, and you have
overcome the evil one.*

(1 JOHN 2:14)

Applying God's promises

He provides food for those who fear him; he remembers his covenant forever.
(PSALM 111:5)

At the time the Spirit of God made such an application of [God's] promises to my mind, and so revealed their real meaning, as to lead me to understand better how to use them, and to what cases they were especially applicable, than I had ever understood before. . . . I had very frequently had the promises so applied, had so applied and used them, as to find that they had a much wider application in their spirit than a mere critical examination of their letter would have warranted.

Charles G. Finney

15.1

Honor him for his works

*Your word, O LORD, is eternal; it stands firm
in the heavens. Your faithfulness continues
through all generations; you established the
earth, and it endures.*
(PSALM 119:89-90)

The laws of God, which are the commentaries of his
works, show them to be yours: because they teach
you to love God with all your soul, and with all your
might. Whom if you love with all the endless powers
of your soul, you will love him in himself, in his
attributes, in his counsels, in all his works, in all his
ways; and in every kind of thing wherein he
appeareth, you will prize him, you will honor him,
you will delight in him, you will ever desire to be
with him and to please him. For to love him in-
cludeth all things. You will feed with pleasure upon
everything that is his. So that the world shall be a
grand jewel of delight unto you: a very paradise and
the gate of heaven.

Thomas Traherne

Trust God's Word—
not your feelings

*Trust in the LORD with all your heart and
lean not on your own understanding;
in all your ways acknowledge him,
and he will make your paths straight.*
(PROVERBS 3:5-6)

Brother, thou desirest to have a sensible feeling of
thy justification; that is, thou wouldst have such a
feeling of God's favor as thou hast of thine own sin.
But that will not be. Yet thy righteousness ought to
surmount all feelings of sin; that is to say, thy righteousness or justification, whereupon thou holdest,
standeth not upon thine own feelings, but upon thy
hoping it shall be revealed when it pleaseth the Lord.
Wherefore thou must not judge according to the
feeling of sin which troubleth and terrifieth thee, but
according to the promise and doctrine of faith,
whereby Christ is promised unto thee, who is thy
perfect and everlasting righteousness.

Martin Luther

15.3

Spiritual illumination

But when he, the Spirit of truth, comes, he will
guide you into all truth. He will not speak on
his own; he will speak only what he hears,
and he will tell you what is yet to come.

(JOHN 16:13)

When the Holy Ghost worketh upon us, and in us, in order to a new creation, he first touched our understanding, that great peace of the heart, with his spiritual illumination. His first word, in order to our conversion is, Let there be light: light, to see their state by nature; light to see the fruits and effects of sin; light, to see the truth and worth of the merits of Jesus Christ; light to see the truth and faithfulness of God, in keeping promise and covenant with them that embrace salvation upon the blessed terms of the gospel of peace.

John Bunyan

15.4

No cause for fear

*There is no fear in love. But perfect love
drives out fear, because fear has to do
with punishment. The one who fears
is not made perfect in love.*

(1 JOHN 4:18)

I . . . call upon you to learn the true and proper
definition of Christ out of these words of Paul,
"which gave himself for our sins." If he gave himself
to death for our sins, then undoubtedly he is no
tyrant or judge which will condemn us for our sins.
He is no caster-down of the afflicted, but a raiser-up
of those that are fallen, a merciful reliever and com-
forter of the heavy and broken-hearted. . . . Here is
then no fear, but altogether sweetness, joy, peace of
conscience. . . . We teach no new thing, but we
repeat and establish old things, which the apostles
and all godly teachers have taught us. And would to
God we could so teach and establish them that we
might not only have them in our mouth, but also
well grounded in the bottom of our heart.

Martin Luther

15.5

Resign thyself to him

*Everyone who competes in the games goes
into strict training. They do it to get
a crown that will not last; but we do it
to get a crown that will last forever.*
(1 CORINTHIANS 9:25)

Regard not much who is for thee, or against thee,
but mind what thou art about, and take care that
God may be with thee in every thing thou doest.
Have a good conscience, and God will well defend
thee. For whom God will help, no man's perverse-
ness shall be able to hurt. If thou canst be silent and
suffer, without doubt thou shalt see that the Lord
will help thee. He knoweth the time and manner
how to deliver thee, and therefore thou oughtest to
resign thyself unto him. It belongs to God to help,
and to deliver from all confusion. It is often very
profitable to keep us more humble that others know
and rebuke our faults.

Thomas à Kempis

15.6

Doubt is the devil's tool

And you also were included in Christ when you heard the word of truth, the gospel of your salvation. Having believed, you were marked in him with a seal, the promised Holy Spirit.
(EPHESIANS 1:13)

Therefore mark how the devil works, for he attacks nothing but faith. Pagans, the unbelieving, the non-Christians he does not tempt. They cling to him like scales to a fish. But when he sees those who have the Word of God, faith, and the Holy Ghost, he cannot get at them. He well knows that he can never win the victory over them, though they may stumble. He well perceives that even if one falls into gross sin, he is not lost thereby, for he can always rise again. Therefore he realizes that he must try a different method and take away their greatest good. If he can prevail upon the soul and make her doubt whether it is the Word of God, the game is won. For God can work all things for good, however often we may stumble, only if we abide by the pure, true Word of God.

Martin Luther

15.7

LEARNING TO TALK TO GOD

*Call to me and I will answer you
and tell you great and unsearchable
things you do not know.*

(JEREMIAH 33:3)

Prayer—a solemn
service to God

Then he said to his disciples, "The harvest is
plentiful but the workers are few.
Ask the Lord of the harvest, therefore,
to send out workers into his harvest field."
(MATTHEW 9:37-38)

Prayer is a solemn service due to God, an adoration, a worship, an approach to God for some request . . . the expression of some need to him, who supplies all need, and who satisfies all desires; who, as a Father, finds his greatest pleasure in relieving the wants and granting the desires of his children. Prayer is the child's request, not to the winds nor to the world, but to the Father. Prayer is the outstretched arms of the child for the Father's help. Prayer is the child's crying call to the Father's ear, the Father's heart, and to the Father's ability, which the Father is to hear, the Father is to feel, and which the Father is to relieve. Prayer is the seeking of God's great and greatest good, which will not come if we do not pray.

E. M. Bounds

16.1

Benefits of prayer

O people of Zion, who live in Jerusalem,
you will weep no more. How gracious
he will be when you cry for help! As soon
as he hears, he will answer you.

(ISAIAH 30:19)

It is by prayer that we reach those riches that are laid up for us with the heavenly Father. For there is a communion of men with God by which, having entered the heavenly sanctuary, they appeal to him in person concerning his promises in order to experience, where necessity so demands, that what they believed was not vain, although he had promised it in word alone. Therefore we see that to us nothing is promised to be expected from the Lord, which we are not also bidden to ask of him in prayers. So true is it that we dig up by prayer the treasures that were pointed out by the Lord's gospel, and which our faith has gazed upon. Words fail to explain how necessary prayer is, and in how many ways the exercise of prayer is profitable. Surely, with good reason the heavenly Father affirms that the only stronghold of safety is in calling upon his name.

John Calvin

16.2

Servants of God are
early on their knees

*Evening, morning and noon I cry out in
distress, and he hears my voice. He ransoms
me unharmed from the battle waged against
me, even though many oppose me.*
(PSALM 55:17-18)

The men who have done the most for God in this
world have been early on their knees. He who fritters
away the early morning, its opportunity and fresh-
ness, in other pursuits than seeking God will make
poor headway seeking him the rest of the day. If God
is not first in our thoughts and efforts in the morning, he will be in the last place the remainder of the
day. Behind this early rising and early praying is the
ardent desire which presses us into this pursuit after
God. Morning listlessness is the index to a listless
heart. The heart which is behindhand in seeking
God in the morning has lost its relish for God.

E. M. Bounds

16.3

The progress of the church
dependent upon prayer

Again, I tell you that if two of you on earth
agree about anything you ask for, it will be
done for you by my Father in heaven.
(MATTHEW 18:19)

Prayer is an absolute necessity to the proper carrying on of God's work. God has made it so. This must have been the principal reason why in the early church, when the complaint that the widows of certain believers had been neglected in the daily administration of the church's benefits, that the twelve called the disciples together, and told them to look for seven men, "full of the Holy Ghost, and wisdom," whom they would appoint over that benevolent work, adding this important statement, "But we will give ourselves continually to prayer and to the ministry of the Word." They surely realized that the success of the Word and the progress of the church was dependent in a preeminent sense upon their "giving themselves to prayer."

E. M. Bounds

16.4

Prayer is acceptable to God

The LORD is near to all who call on him,
to all who call on him in truth.
He fulfills the desires of those who fear him;
he hears their cry and saves them.
(PSALM 145:18-19)

Prayer is complementary, made efficient and cooperative with God's will, whose sovereign sway is to run parallel in extent and power with the atonement of Jesus Christ. . . . But how do I know that I am praying by the will of God? Every true attempt to pray is in response to the will of God. Bungling it may be, and untutored by human teachers, but it is acceptable to God because it is in obedience to his will. If I will give myself up to the inspiration of the Spirit of God, who commands me to pray, the details and the petitions of that praying will all fall into harmony with the will of him who wills that I should pray.

E. M. Bounds

Prayer and God's purposes
a mighty combination

The Lord God says: "I am ready to hear Israel's prayers for these blessings, and to grant them their requests. Let them but ask and I will multiply them like the flocks that fill Jerusalem's streets at time of sacrifice."
(EZEKIEL 36:37-38 TLB)

The possibilities of prayer are found in its allying itself with the purposes of God, for God's purposes and man's praying are the combination of all potent and omnipotent forces. More than this, the possibilities of prayer are seen in the fact that it changes the purposes of God. It is in the very nature of prayer to plead and give directions. Prayer is not a negation. It is a positive force. It never rebels against the will of God, never comes into conflict with that will, but that it does seek to change God's purpose is evident. Christ said, "The cup which my Father hath given me shall I not drink it?" and yet he had prayed that very night, "If it be possible let this cup pass from me."

E. M. Bounds

16.6

Prayer the noblest exercise

And pray in the Spirit on all occasions
with all kinds of prayers and requests.
With this in mind, be alert and
always keep on praying for all the saints.
(EPHESIANS 6:18)

Prayer . . . is the noblest exercise of the soul, and the most exalted use of our best faculties, and the highest imitation of the blessed inhabitants of heaven. . . . On the other hand, sleep is the poorest, dullest refreshment of the body . . . that we are forced to receive it either in a state of insensibility or in the folly of dreams. . . . Even animals amongst mere animals, we despise them most which are most drowsy. He, therefore, that chooses to enlarge the slothful indulgence of sleep rather than be early at his devotions to God chooses the dullest refreshment of the body before the highest, noblest employment of the soul; he chooses a state which is a reproach to mere animals rather than that exercise which is the glory of angels.

William Law

PRAYER IS ESSENTIAL TO CHRISTIAN LIVING

Ask and it will be given to you; seek and you will find; knock and the door will be opened to you. For everyone who asks receives; he who seeks finds; and to him who knocks, the door will be opened.

(MATTHEW 7:7-8)

Feeble living, debilitated praying

*But when you pray, go into your room,
close the door and pray to your Father,
who is unseen. Then your Father, who sees what
is done in secret, will reward you. And when
you pray, do not keep on babbling like pagans,
for they think they will be heard because of their
many words. Do not be like them, for your
Father knows what you need before you ask him.*
(MATTHEW 6:6-8)

Feebleness of living reflects its debility and languor
in the praying hours. We simply cannot talk to God
strongly, intimately, and confidently unless we are
living for him, faithfully and truly. The prayer-closet
cannot become sanctified unto God, when the life is
alien to his precepts and purpose. We must learn this
lesson well—the righteous character and Christlike
conduct give us a peculiar and preferential standing
in prayer before God.

E. M. Bounds

Spiritually minded
people love God

May the words of my mouth and the meditation of my heart be pleasing in your sight, O LORD, my Rock and my Redeemer.
(PSALM 19:14)

Spiritually minded people love God, not for the benefits he gives but for the excellence of himself and the beauty of what he does. They love Jesus Christ who is uniquely God in human form. They love all spiritual things because the presence of God is made known by them. They love all Bible truth, for it is God's Word to them. One evidence, therefore, of genuine spiritual renewal in people is that the whole of them is affected by it, and they then are devoted to everything spiritual. There is a universality, both subjective and objective, about the genuine experience of spiritual mindedness.

John Owen

An unfathomable mystery

Just as each of us has one body with many
members, and these members do not all have
the same function, so in Christ
we who are many form one body,
and each member belongs to all the others.
(ROMANS 12:4-5)

This perfect harmony and union of Divine Sovereignty and human liberty is to us an unfathomable mystery. . . . But let it be our comfort and strength to be assured that in the eternal fellowship of the Father and the Son the power of prayer has its origin and certainty, and that through our union with the Son our prayer is taken up and can have its influence in the inner life of the Blessed Trinity. God's decrees are not iron framework against which man's liberty would vainly seek to struggle. No, God himself is the Living Love, who in his Son as man has entered into the tenderest relationship with all that is human, who through the Holy Spirit . . . keeps himself free to give every human prayer its place in his government of the world.

Andrew Murray

17.3

Let nothing hinder prayer

*The Lord has set apart the redeemed for
himself. Therefore he will listen to me
and answer when I call to him.*
(PSALM 4:3, TLB)

Sacred work—church activities—may so engage and
absorb us as to hinder praying, and when this is the
case, evil results always follow. It is better to let the
work go by default than to let the praying go by
neglect. Whatever affects the intensity of our prayer
affects the value of our work. "Too busy to pray" is
not only the keynote to backsliding, but it mars even
the work done. Nothing is well done without prayer
for the simple reason that it leaves God out of the
account. . . . How easy to neglect prayer or abbrevi-
ate our praying simply by the plea that we have
church work on our hands. Satan has effectively
disarmed us when he can keep us too busy doing
things to stop and pray.

E. M. Bounds

17.4

The Christian life
is spiritual warfare

We are not fighting against people made of flesh and blood, but against persons without bodies—the evil rulers of the unseen world, those mighty satanic beings and great evil princes of darkness who rule this world; and against huge numbers of wicked spirits in the spirit world.

(EPHESIANS 6:12, TLB)

It cannot be stated too frequently that the life of a Christian is a warfare, an intense conflict, a lifelong contest. It is a battle, moreover, waged against invisible foes, who are ever alert, and ever seeking to entrap, deceive, and ruin the souls of men. The life to which Holy Scripture calls me is no picnic, or holiday junketing. . . . It entails effort, wrestling, struggling; it demands the putting forth of the full energy of the spirit in order to frustrate the foe and to come off, at the last, more than conqueror. . . . From start to finish, it is war. From the hour in which he first draws sword, to that in which he doffs his harness, the Christian warrior is compelled to "endure hardness like a good soldier."

E. M. Bounds

17.5

Think in a godly way

*"For who has known the mind of the Lord
that he may instruct him?"
But we have the mind of Christ.*
(1 Corinthians 2:16)

We must not forget that by ourselves we cannot
properly think of spiritual things. We must not suppose that our thoughts are our own and therefore we
can do what we want to with them. Paul's advice is
good—we need God's help in order to be able to
think in a godly way (2 Corinthians 3:5). One may
be able to think theologically, using natural reason,
but if there is no delight in the things being thought
about, and no holiness of life arising from them,
such thinking is not spiritual mindedness. Natural
resources cannot produce spirituality.

John Owen

17.6

Spiritual mindedness:
The mark of a believer

The mind of sinful man is death, but the
mind controlled by the Spirit is life and peace.
(ROMANS 8:6)

Spiritual mindedness consists of three things; the mind always actively directing thoughts to spiritual things; a growing love for spiritual things; a real sense of satisfaction experienced by the believer which is produced by spiritual things. Paul makes the point that this spiritual mindedness is the chief distinguishing mark of a believer and that it alone leads to life and peace. Then how vital it must be!

John Owen

GOD'S CHILDREN ARE PRODUCTIVE

Remain in me, and I will remain in you. No branch can bear fruit by itself; it must remain in the vine. Neither can you bear fruit unless you remain in me.

(JOHN 15:4)

We should bear fruit

They will come and shout for joy on the heights
of Zion; they will rejoice in the bounty of the
LORD—the grain, the new wine and the oil,
the young of the flocks and herds.
They will be like a well-watered garden,
and they will sorrow no more.
(JEREMIAH 31:12)

In our Lord's language to his disciples about choosing them that they should bear fruit, he clearly teaches us that this matter of praying and fruit-bearing is not a petty business of our choice, or a secondary matter in relation to other matters, but that he has chosen us for this very business of praying. He had especially in mind our praying and . . . he expects us to do . . . it intelligently and well. For he before says that he had made us his friends, and had brought us into bosom confidence with him and also into free and full conference with him. The main object of choosing us as his disciples and of friendship with him was that we might be the better fitted to bear the fruit of prayer.

E. M. Bounds

18.1

Lack of ardor, a sure sign
of shallowness

Therefore, my dear brothers, stand firm.
Let nothing move you. Always give yourselves
fully to the work of the Lord, because you know
that your labor in the Lord is not in vain.
(1 CORINTHIANS 15:58)

A lack of ardor in prayer is the sure sign of a lack of depth and of intensity of desire; and the absence of intense desire is a sure sign of God's absence from the heart! To abate fervor is to retire from God. He can and will pardon sin when the penitent pray, but two things are intolerable to him—insincerity and lukewarmness. Lack of heart and lack of heat are two things he loathes, and to the Laodiceans he said, in terms of unmistakable severity and condemnation: "I would thou wert cold or hot. So then because thou art lukewarm, and neither cold nor hot, I will spue thee out of my mouth." This was God's expressed judgment on the lack of fire in one of the seven churches, and it is his indictment against individual Christians for the fatal want of sacred zeal.

E. M. Bounds

18.2

To keep the soul
from drying up

*He is like a tree planted by streams of water,
which yields its fruit in season and whose leaf
does not wither. Whatever he does prospers.*

(PSALM 1:3)

Just as all streams are clear which issue from a clear
spring, so is a soul in a state of grace. Because the
streams proceed from this fount of life, a fount in
which the soul is planted like a tree, they are most
pleasing in the eyes of both God and man. But there
would be no refreshment, no fruitage, if it were not
from this fount sustaining the tree of the righteous
man. This fount keeps the soul from drying up, and
helps it to produce good fruit. In contrast, the soul
that deliberately separates itself from this fount can
only be planted in a pool of foul and stagnant water
from which flow equally foul and fetid streams.

Teresa of Avila

Prayerless souls are like paralyzed bodies

I am the vine; you are the branches.
If a man remains in me and I in him,
he will bear much fruit;
apart from me you can do nothing.
(JOHN 15:5)

A very learned man once told me that souls without the exercise of prayer are like a body that is paralyzed or crippled. Although it has hands and feet, it cannot use them. In the same way there are some souls that are so weak, and so caught up in external affairs, that they have no idea how they can enter into themselves. . . . Although they have been given a nature which is so richly endowed that they are able to hold communion even with God himself, yet there is no remedy for them. Like Lot's wife, who looked back and was turned into a pillar of salt, so these souls that do not strive to understand and to amend their miserable condition will likewise be changed into pillars of salt.

Teresa of Avila

18.4

Discover the power
of believing prayer

The righteous cry out, and the LORD hears them; he delivers them from all their troubles.
(PSALM 34:17)

When once faith has taken its stand on God's Word and the Name of Jesus, and has yielded itself to the leading of the Spirit to seek God's will and honor alone in its prayer, it need not be discouraged by delay. It knows from Scripture that the power of believing prayer is simply irresistible; real faith can never be disappointed. It knows that just as water, to exercise the irresistible power it can have, must be gathered up and accumulated until the stream can come down in full force, so there must often be a heaping up of prayer until God sees that the measure is full, when the answer comes.

Andrew Murray

The devil knows the power
of our prayers

The LORD is far from the wicked
but he hears the prayer of the righteous.
(PROVERBS 15:29)

When any for relief run to confess, the only true remedy for them is prayer; to present themselves before God as criminals, beg strength of him to rise out of this state. . . . But the devil has falsely persuaded the doctors and the wise men of the age, that, in order to pray, it is necessary first to be perfectly converted. . . . The devil is outrageous only against prayer, and those who exercise it; because he knows it is the true means of taking his prey from him. He lets us undergo all the austerities we will. He neither persecutes those who enjoy them nor those that practice them. But no sooner does one enter into a spiritual life, a life of prayer, but they must prepare for strange crosses. All manner of persecutions and contempts in this world are reserved for that life.

Jeanne Guyon

18.6

Prayer is the faithful sentinel

Because the Sovereign LORD helps me,
I will not be disgraced. Therefore have
I set my face like flint,
and I know I will not be put to shame.
(ISAIAH 50:7)

One of Satan's wiliest tricks is to destroy the best by
the good. Business and other duties are good, but
we are so filled with these that they crowd out and
destroy the best. Prayer holds the citadel for God,
and if Satan can by any means weaken prayer he is a
gainer so far, and when prayer is dead the citadel is
taken. We must keep prayer as the faithful sentinel
keeps guard, with sleepless vigilance. We must not
keep it half-starved and feeble as a baby, but we
must keep it in giant strength. Our prayer-chamber
should have our freshest strength, our calmest time,
its hours unfettered, without obtrusion, without
haste. Private place and plenty of time are the life of
prayer.

E. M. Bounds

18.7

GOD'S PROMISED HELP

*Yet the LORD longs to be gracious to
you; he rises to show you compassion.
For the LORD is a God of justice.
Blessed are all who wait for him!*

(ISAIAH 30:18)

19.0

Great and precious promises

*No one whose hope is in you will ever be
put to shame, but they will be put to shame
who are treacherous without excuse.*
(PSALM 25:3)

The promises of God are "exceeding great and precious," words which clearly indicate their great value and their broad reach, as grounds upon which to base our expectations in praying. Howsoever exceeding great and precious they are, their realization . . . is based on prayer. How glorious are these promises to the believing saints and to the whole church! . . . Yet these promises never brought hope to bloom or fruit to a prayerless heart. Neither could these promises, were they a thousandfold, increased in number and preciousness, bring millennium glory to a prayerless church. Prayer makes the promise rich, fruitful, and a conscious reality.

E. M. Bounds

"Ask, seek, knock"

Blessed is he . . . whose hope is in the LORD, his
God, the Maker of heaven and earth,
the sea, and everything in them—the LORD,
who remains faithful forever.
(PSALM 146:5-6)

God holds all good in his hands. That good comes
to us through our Lord Jesus Christ because of his
all atoning merits, by asking it in his name. The only
and the sole command in which all the others of its
class belong is, "Ask, seek, knock." And the one and
sole promise is its counterpart, its necessary equiva-
lent and results: "It shall be given—ye shall find—it
shall be opened unto you." God is so much involved
in prayer and its hearing and answering, that all of
his attributes and his whole being are centered in
that great fact. It distinguishes him as peculiarly
beneficent, wonderfully good, and powerfully attractive in his nature. "O thou that hearest prayer!
To thee shall all flesh come."

E. M. Bounds

19.2

Count on the promises of God

This is the confidence we have in
approaching God: that if we ask anything
according to his will, he hears us.
(1 JOHN 5:14)

How vast are the possibilities of prayer! How wide is its reach! What great things are accomplished by this divinely appointed means of grace! It lays its hand on Almighty God and moves him to do what he would not otherwise do if prayer was not offered. It brings things to pass which would never otherwise occur. The story of prayer is the story of great achievements. Prayer is a wonderful power placed by Almighty God in the hands of his saints, which may be used to accomplish great purposes and to achieve unusual results. Prayer reaches to everything, takes in all things great and small which are promised by God to the children of men. The only limit to prayer are the promises of God and his ability to fulfill those promises.

E. M. Bounds

19.3

Cultivate the habit
of spiritual thinking

*But the wisdom that comes from heaven is first
of all pure; then peace-loving, considerate,
submissive, full of mercy and good fruit,
impartial and sincere.*
(JAMES 3:17)

Some may suggest that if we really try to live spiritually, then it will be impossible for us to find time to do anything else—no time will be left for lawful employment and leisure! There have been those who withdrew from normal life in the mistaken belief that this was essential to spirituality. But spiritual mindedness does not mean withdrawing from life; it means bringing spirituality into every part of it. . . . I repeat that believers who do not cultivate the habit of spiritual thinking will not enjoy life and peace.

John Owen

Prepare a reverent attitude

We have not received the spirit of the world but the Spirit who is from God, that we may understand what God has freely given us.
(1 CORINTHIANS 2:12)

A spiritual attitude of mind is no hindrance to secular work: even though a pot is full of chaff (the secular) you can still pour a lot of water (the spiritual) into the same space. In order to preserve one's spirituality while occupied with secular matters, it is vital to have some time in the day set apart for prayer and Bible reading. Such times should be regular, or other matters may crowd them out of your life. Choose a time when you are most alert—we should serve God with the best that we can be (Malachi 1:8). Prepare yourself to have a reverent attitude of mind. Seek to have an earnest desire to spend your time in this way: don't let it be a tiresome duty.

John Owen

Be delighted by
spiritual things

Accept, O LORD, the willing praise
of my mouth, and teach me your laws.
Though I constantly take my life
in my hands, I will not forget your law.
(PSALM 119:108-109)

Spiritual mindedness grows from and consists of being delighted by spiritual things: what we love is what captures us. The great contest between heaven and earth is to see which of them can most draw out our love. Whoever has our love has the whole of us; love causes us to give ourselves away, as nothing else can. Our love is like the rudder of a ship—where it is turned, there the ship goes.

John Owen

Develop a strong attachment to spiritual things

For God, who said, "Let light shine out of darkness," made his light shine in our hearts to give us the light of the knowledge of the glory of God in the face of Christ.
(2 CORINTHIANS 4:6)

The attitude that believers have toward the things of this world is a good indicator of whether they are spiritually minded or not. No one can have a detached attitude to the things of this life unless there is a strong attachment to spiritual things. To think less of anything one must think more of something else. Our love for the things of this world needs to be strictly disciplined. How can we love what God has shown to be contemptible? Our love for this world will not fade away of its own accord. We must deliberately keep it from governing us. We are to be governed by God's Word alone (1 John 2:5).

John Owen

Week Twenty

KEEP SEEKING IN DRY TIMES

The poor will see and be glad—
you who seek God, may your hearts live!

(PSALM 69:32)

20.0

The King assumes
the responsibility

*Then you will call upon me and come
and pray to me, and I will listen to you.*
(JEREMIAH 29:12)

To pray in the name of Christ means I dare not
approach God without a mediator. . . . When a magistrate gives a command in the name of the king, it
naturally follows that what he commands must be
the king's will; he cannot command his own will in
the king's name. The same thing is true of praying
in the name of Jesus; to pray in such a way that it is
in conformity with the will of Jesus. I cannot pray in
the name of Jesus to have my own will. . . . Finally,
when a magistrate gives an order in the name of the
king, it means that the king assumes the responsibility. So too with prayer in the name of Jesus, Jesus
assumes the responsibility and all the consequences.
He steps forward for us, steps into the place of the
person praying.

Søren Kierkegaard

Don't be discouraged
by distractions

*Let us draw near to God with a sincere heart
in full assurance of faith, having our hearts
sprinkled to cleanse us from a guilty
conscience and having our bodies washed with
pure water. Let us hold unswervingly to the
hope we profess, for he who promised is
faithful. And let us consider how we may spur
one another on toward love and good deeds.*
(HEBREWS 10:22-24)

When you see your mind wandering [during prayer], bring it back gently without being upset, and without ever being discouraged by these distractions which are stubborn. On the contrary, they will help you more than a prayer which brings with it very evident comfort and fervor, because these distractions will humble you, mortify you, and accustom you to seek God purely for his own sake, unmixed with any pleasure.

Fénelon

20.2

Repentance: He is ready
to receive

*They will come with weeping; they will pray
as I bring them back. I will lead them beside
streams of water on a level path
where they will not stumble.*

(JEREMIAH 31:9)

O sinner, sinner! hast thou any reason to complain
of God? If there yet remains in thee any justice,
confess the truth, and admit that it is owing to
thyself if thou goest wrong; that in departing from
him thou disobeyest his call. When thou returnest,
he is ready to receive thee; and if thou returnest not,
he makes use of the most engaging motives to win
thee. Yet thou turnest a deaf ear to his voice; thou
wilt not hear him. Thou sayest he speaks not to thee,
though he calls loudly. It is therefore only because
thou daily rebellest, and art growing daily more and
more deaf to the voice.

Jeanne Guyon

20.3

Prayer in dry season
not offered in vain

O God, you are my God, earnestly I seek you;
my soul thirsts for you, my body longs for you,
in a dry and weary land
where there is no water.
(PSALM 63:1)

I have since experienced, that the prayer of the heart when it appears most dry and barren, nevertheless is not ineffectual nor offered in vain. God gives what is best for us, though not what we most relish or wish for. Were people but convinced of this truth, they would be far from complaining all their lives. By causing us death he would procure us life; for all our happiness, spiritual, temporal, and eternal, consists in resigning ourselves to God, leaving it to him to do in us and with us as he pleases, and with so much the more submission; as things please us less.

Jeanne Guyon

Persevere to the end

Since you have kept my command to endure patiently, I will also keep you from the hour of trial that is going to come upon the whole world to test those who live on the earth.

(REVELATION 3:10)

We seek excuses, saying that we fear to have lost God when we are no longer conscious of him. But in truth, it is our own impatience under trial; it is the restlessness of our hypersensitive and self-centered nature; it is the seeking of some support for our self-love, it is an inertia toward abandon, and a secret revival of ourself after having been freed by grace. My God, where are the souls that do not stop on the way of death? Those who persevere to the end will be crowned.

Fénelon

A thirst only God can fill

Blessed are those who hunger and thirst for righteousness, for they will be filled.
(MATTHEW 5:6)

What meaneth this restlessness of our nature? . . .
What mean those unmeasurable longings which no
gratification can extinguish, and which still continue
to agitate the heart of man, even in the fullness of
plenty and of enjoyment? If they mean anything at
all, they mean that all which this world can offer is
not enough to fill up his capacity for happiness—that
time is too small for him and he is born for something beyond it—that the scene of his earthly existence is too limited and he is formed to expiate in a
wider and a grander theater—that a nobler destiny is
reserved for him—and that to accomplish the purpose of his being he must soar above the littleness of
the world and aim at a loftier prize.

Thomas Chalmer

God doesn't forget us

When Jacob awoke from his sleep, he thought,
"Surely the LORD is in this place,
and I was not aware of it."
(GENESIS 28:16)

When God wants to strengthen a man's faith he first
weakens it by feigning to break faith with him. He
thrusts him into many tribulations and makes him so
weary that he is driven to despair, and yet he gives
him strength to be still and persevere. Such quietness is patience, and patience produces experience,
so that when God returns to him and lets his sun rise
and shine again, and when the storm is over he
opens his eyes in amazement and says: "The Lord
shall be praised, that I have been delivered from evil.
God dwells here. I did not think that all would end
so well."

Martin Luther

Week Twenty-One

PRAYER: STRENGTH FOR THE JOURNEY

Be still before the LORD and wait patiently for him; do not fret when men succeed in their ways, when they carry out their wicked schemes.

(PSALM 37:7)

True prayer takes more time

The LORD is good to those whose hope is in him, to the one who seeks him; it is good to wait quietly for the salvation of the LORD.
(LAMENTATIONS 3:25-26)

The secret for much mischief to our own souls, and to the souls of others, lies in the way that we stint, and starve, and scamp our prayers, by hurrying over them. Prayer worth calling prayer; prayer that God will call true prayer and will treat as true prayer, takes far more time, by the clock, than one man in a thousand thinks. As long as we remain in this unspiritual and undevotional world, we shall not succeed . . . in prayer without time, and times, and places, and other assistances in prayer. . . . If you find your life of prayer to be always so short, and so easy, and so spiritual, as to be without cost and strain and sweat to you, you may depend upon it, you are not begun to pray.

Alexander Whyte

21.1

The answer is near,
even at the door

Be patient, then, brothers, until the Lord's
coming. See how the farmer waits for the land
to yield its valuable crop and how patient he is
for the autumn and spring rains.
You too, be patient and stand firm,
because the Lord's coming is near.
(JAMES 5:7-8)

I cannot tell how absurd unbelief looked to me, and how certain it was in my mind that God would answer prayer, and those prayers that from day to day and from hour to hour I found myself offering in such agony and faith. I had no idea in my mind of the shape the answer would take, the locality in which the prayers would be answered, or the exact time of the answer. My impression was that the answer was near, even at the door; and I felt myself strengthened in the divine life, put on the harness for a mighty conflict with the powers of darkness, and expected soon to see a far more powerful outpouring of the Spirit of God in that new country where I had been laboring.

Charles G. Finney

21.2

The need for absolute dependence on God

Yes, LORD, walking in the way of your laws,
we wait for you; your name and
renown are the desire of our hearts.
(ISAIAH 26:8)

Just as there is but one God, who is a Spirit, who hears prayer, there is but one spirit of acceptable prayer. When we realize what time Christ spent in prayer, and how the great events of his life were all connected with special prayer, we learn the necessity of absolute dependence on and unceasing direct communication with the heavenly world, if we are to live a heavenly life, or to exercise heavenly power around us. We see how foolish and fruitless the attempt must be to do work for God and heaven, without, in the first place, being in prayer, getting the life and the power of leave to possess us. Unless this truth lives in us, we cannot avail ourselves aright of the mighty power of the name of Christ.

Andrew Murray

Learn to give God time

Let us not become weary in doing good,
for at the proper time we will
reap a harvest if we do not give up.
(GALATIANS 6:9)

Our great danger . . . is the temptation to think that
. . . it may not be God's will to give us what we ask.
If our prayer be according to God's Word, and
under the leading of the Spirit, let us not give way
to these fears. Let us learn to give God time. God
needs time with us. If only we give him time, that is,
time in the daily fellowship with himself, for him to
exercise the full influence of his presence on us, and
time, day by day, in the course of our being kept
waiting, for faith to prove its reality and to fill our
whole being, he himself will lead us from faith to
vision; we shall see the glory of God.

Andrew Murray

Prayer brings subjection
to the will of God

*O my people in Jerusalem, you shall weep no
more, for he will surely be gracious to you at
the sound of your cry. He will answer you.*
(ISAIAH 30:19, TLB)

Prayer in the time of trouble tends to bring the spirit
into perfect subjection to the will of God, to cause
the will to be conformed to God's will, and saves
from all murmurings over our lot, and delivers from
everything like a rebellious heart or a spirit critical of
the Lord. Prayer sanctifies trouble to our highest
good. Prayer so prepares the heart that it softens
under the disciplining hand of God. Prayer places us
where God can bring to us the greatest good, spiritual and eternal. Prayer allows God to freely work
with us and in us in the day of trouble. Prayer
removes everything in the way of trouble, bringing
to us the sweetest, the highest and greatest good.
Prayer permits God's servant, trouble, to accomplish its mission in us, with us and for us.

E. M. Bounds

21.5

Never lose courage;
wait with patience

I will wait for the LORD, who is hiding
his face from the house of Jacob.
I will put my trust in him.
(ISAIAH 8:17)

In all our spiritual dryness and barrenness let us never lose courage but, waiting with patience for the return of consolation, earnestly pursue our course. Let us not omit any of our exercises of devotion, but if possible let us multiply our good works; and not being able to present liquid sweetmeats to our dear Spouse, let us offer him dry ones; for it is all one to him, if only the heart which offers them is perfectly fixed on the resolution of loving him. . . . It is no such great matter to serve a prince in the quietness of a time of peace and amongst the delights of the court; but to serve him amidst the hardships of war, in troubles and persecutions, is a true mark of constancy and fidelity.

Francis de Sales

Wait on God

For the revelation awaits an appointed time;
it speaks of the end and will not prove false.
Though it linger, wait for it;
it will certainly come and will not delay.
(HABAKKUK 2:3)

Some people want to show God the goal and to determine the time and manner and at the same time suggest how they wish to be helped; and if things do not turn out as they wish, they become faint-hearted, or, if they can, they seek help elsewhere. They do not wait upon God, rather God should wait for them and be ready at once to help them in the way they have planned. But those who truly wait upon God ask for grace, and they leave it free to God's good pleasure how, where, and by what means he shall help them. They do not despair of help, yet they do not give it a name. They rather leave it to God to baptize and name it, however long it may be delayed.

Martin Luther

21.7

UNDERSTANDING THE MEANING OF SUFFERING

Be self-controlled and alert. Your enemy the devil prowls around like a roaring lion looking for someone to devour. Resist him, standing firm in the faith, because you know that your brothers throughout the world are undergoing the same kind of sufferings. And the God of all grace, who called you to his eternal glory in Christ, after you have suffered a little while, will himself restore you and make you strong, firm and steadfast.

(1 PETER 5:8-10)

Bearers of his cross

To this you were called, because Christ
suffered for you, leaving you an example,
that you should follow in his steps.
(1 PETER 2:21)

Jesus hath now many lovers of the heavenly kingdom, but few bearers of his Cross. He hath many desirous of consolation, but few of tribulation. He findeth many companions of his table, but few of his abstinence. All desire to rejoice with him, few are willing to endure anything for him, or with him. . . . But they who love Jesus for the sake of Jesus, and not for some special comfort of their own, bless him in all tribulations and anguish of heart as well as in the state of highest comfort. Yea, although he should never be willing to give them comfort, they notwithstanding would ever praise him, and wish to be always giving thanks. O how perfect is the pure love of Jesus, which is mixed with no self-interest or self love! Are not all those to be called mercenary who are ever seeking consolations?

Thomas à Kempis

Embrace the suffering
God offers

But even if you should suffer for what is right, you are blessed. "Do not fear what they fear; do not be frightened."
(1 PETER 3:14)

Do not anticipate crosses. You would perhaps seek some that God would not want to give you, and some that would be incompatible with his plans for you. But embrace without hesitation all those that his hand offers you every moment. There is a providence for crosses, as for the necessities of life. It is the daily bread that feeds the soul and which God never fails to distribute to you.

Fénelon

22.2

Expect to meet with trials

Dear friends, do not be surprised at the painful trial you are suffering, as though something strange were happening to you. But rejoice that you participate in the sufferings of Christ, so that you may be overjoyed when his glory is revealed.
(1 PETER 4:12-13)

Since "man is born unto trouble as the sparks fly upward," (Job 5:7) and Adam has entailed on all his race the sad inheritance of calamity in their way to death, it will certainly be prudent and necessary, that we should all expect to meet with trials and afflictions; and that you, reader, whoever you are, should be endeavoring to gird on your armor, and put yourself in a posture to encounter those trials which will fall to your lot as a man and a Christian. Prepare yourself to receive your afflictions, and to endure them, in a manner agreeable to both these characters. . . . When at length your turn comes, as it certainly will, from the first hour in which an affliction seizes you, realize to yourself the hand of God in it.

Philip Doddridge

22.3

Prepare to confront injustice and suffering

If you are insulted because of the name of Christ, you are blessed, for the Spirit of glory and of God rests on you.
(1 PETER 4:14)

No one is responsible for all the injustice and suffering in the world, and no one wants to set himself up as the judge of the world. Psychologically, our lack of imagination, of sensitivity, and of mental alertness is balanced by a steady composure, an ability to go on working, and a great capacity for suffering. But from a Christian point of view, none of these excuses can obscure the fact that the most important factor, large-heartedness, is lacking. Christ kept himself from suffering till his hour had come, but when it did come he met it as a free man, seized it, and mastered it.

Dietrich Bonhoeffer

22.4

Imitate the passion of Christ

Therefore, since Christ suffered in his body,
arm yourselves also with the same attitude,
because he who has suffered
in his body is done with sin.
(1 PETER 4:1)

All the ends of the earth, all the kingdoms of the world would be of no profit to me; as far as I am concerned, to die in Jesus Christ is better than to be a monarch of earth's widest bounds. He who died for us is all that I seek; He who rose again for us is my whole desire. The pangs of birth are upon me; have patience with me, my brothers, and do not shut me out from life, do not wish me to be stillborn. Here is one who only longs to be God's; do not make a present of him to the world again, or delude him with the things of earth. Suffer me to attain to light, light pure and undefiled; for only when I am come thither shall I be truly a man. Leave me to imitate the Passion of my God. If any of you has God within himself, let that man understand my longings and feel for me, because he will know the forces by which I am constrained.

Ignatius of Antioch

22.5

Be willing to suffer with Christ

When they hurled their insults at him,
he did not retaliate; when he suffered,
he made no threats. Instead, he entrusted
himself to him who judges justly.
(1 PETER 2:23)

It is infinitely easier to suffer in obedience to a human command than to accept suffering as free, responsible men. It is infinitely easier to suffer with others than to suffer alone. It is infinitely easier to suffer as public heroes than to suffer apart and in ignominy. It is infinitely easier to suffer physical death than to endure spiritual suffering. Christ suffered as a free man alone, apart and in ignominy, in body and in spirit, and since that day many Christians have suffered with him.

Dietrich Bonhoeffer

22.6

Christic fights at our side

*No temptation has seized you except what is
common to man. And God is faithful;
he will not let you be tempted beyond what you
can bear. But when you are tempted,
he will also provide a way out
so that you can stand up under it.*
(1 CORINTHIANS 10:13)

Our life is a continual combat, but a combat in
which Jesus Christ fights with us. We must let temptation rage around us and not cease to go forward;
as a traveler, surprised by a great wind on a plain,
wraps his cloak around him and goes always on
despite the bad weather.

Fénelon

WILLINGNESS TO SUFFER AND DIE

During the days of Jesus' life on earth, he offered up prayers and petitions with loud cries and tears to the one who could save him from death, and he was heard because of his reverent submission. Although he was a son, he learned obedience from what he suffered and, once made perfect, he became the source of eternal salvation for all who obey him.

(HEBREWS 5:7-9)

23.0

We belong to Jesus Christ

If you suffer as a Christian,
do not be ashamed, but praise
God that you bear that name.
(1 PETER 4:16)

Many who pray for humility would be extremely sorry if God were to grant it to them. This is one of the points on which people are most easily deluded. Some book, or meditation . . . touches their heart; they feel the attraction of this virtue, and ask God to give it to them; but they forget that to love, desire, and ask for humility is loving, desiring, and asking for humiliations. . . . Without them it is no more than a beautiful but meaningless idea. . . . But there are truly those, though not very many, who . . . offer themselves to carry all the humiliating crosses that he is pleased to send them. . . . From that moment they should feel that they are not their own, but belong to Jesus Christ and are fighting under his standard.

Jean Nicolas Grou

23.1

Suffer for righteousness' sake

Remember those earlier days after you had
received the light, when you stood your ground
in a great contest in the face of suffering.
(HEBREWS 10:32)

Dost thou suffer for righteousness' sake? Why then, thy righteousness is not diminished, but rather increased by thy sufferings. Righteousness thriveth best in affliction, the more afflicted, the more holy man; the more persecuted, the more shining man. The prison is the furnace, thy graces are the silver and the gold; wherefore, as the silver and the gold are refined by the fire, and so made more to show their native brightness, so the Christian that hath, and that loveth righteousness, and that suffereth for its sake, is by his sufferings refined and made more righteous, and made more Christian, more godly. Some indeed, when they come there, prove lead, iron, tin, and the best, but the dross of silver; and so are fit for nothing, but there to be left and consumed.

John Bunyan

We lose our life to save it

Whoever finds his life will lose it, and whoever loses his life for my sake will find it.
(MATTHEW 10:39)

The Christian believes that in Christ he has died, yet he is more alive than before, and he fully expects to live forever. He walks on earth while seated in heaven, and though born on earth he finds that after his conversion he is not at home here. Like the nighthawk, which in the air is the essence of grace and beauty but on the ground is awkward and ugly, so the Christian appears at his best in the heavenly places but does not fit well into the ways of the very society into which he was born. The Christian soon learns that if he would be victorious as a son of heaven among men on earth, he must not follow the common pattern of mankind, but rather the contrary. That he may be safe he puts himself in jeopardy; he loses his life to save it and is in danger of losing it if he attempts to preserve it.

A. W. Tozer

Immoderate attachments

Do not love the world or anything in the world.
If anyone loves the world, the love of the Father
is not in him. For everything in the world—the
cravings of sinful man, the lust of his eyes and
the boasting of what he has and does—comes not
from the Father but from the world.

(1 JOHN 2:15-16)

They, then, who lost their worldly all in the sack of Rome, if they owned their possessions as they had been taught by the apostle, who himself was poor without but rich within—that is to say, if they used the world as not using it—could say with Job . . . "Naked came I out of my mother's womb, and naked shall I return thither: the Lord gave, and the Lord hath taken away; as it pleased the Lord, so has it come to pass: blessed be the name of the Lord." . . . But as to those feebler spirits who, though they cannot be said to prefer earthly possessions to Christ, do yet cleave to them with a somewhat immoderate attachment, they have discovered by the pain of losing them how much they were sinning in loving them. For their grief is of their own making.

Augustine of Hippo

23.4

Instruments in the hand of the Lord

*For just as the sufferings of Christ flow over
into our lives, so also through
Christ our comfort overflows.*

(2 CORINTHIANS 1:5)

We are certainly not Christ; we are not called on to redeem the world by our own deeds and sufferings, and we need not try to assume such an impossible burden. We are not lords, but instruments in the hand of the Lord of history; and we can share in other people's suffering only to a very limited degree. We are not Christ, but if we want to be Christians, we must have some share in Christ's large heartedness by acting with responsibility and in freedom when the hour of danger comes, and by showing a real sympathy that springs, not from fear, but from liberating and redeeming love of Christ for all who suffer. Mere waiting and looking is not Christian behavior. The Christian is called to sympathy and action, not in the first place by his own sufferings, but by the sufferings of his brethren, for whose sake Christ suffered.

Dietrich Bonhoeffer

23.5

Follow God; seek to be other-worldly

Then Jesus said to his disciples, "If anyone would come after me, he must deny himself and take up his cross and follow me."
(MATTHEW 16:24)

If we truly want to follow God we must seek to be other-worldly. This I say knowing well that that word has been used with scorn by the sons of this world and applied to the Christian as a badge of reproach. So be it. Every man must choose his world. If we would follow Christ, with all the facts before us and knowing what we are about, deliberately choose the Kingdom of God as our sphere of interest I see no reason why anyone should object. If we lose by it, the loss is our own; if we gain, we rob no one by so doing. The "other world," which is the object of this world's disdain and the subject of the drunkard's mocking song, is our carefully chosen goal and the object of our holiest longing.

A. W. Tozer

23.6

The church will suffer

Dear friends, do not be surprised at the painful trial you are suffering, as though something strange were happening to you. But rejoice that you participate in the sufferings of Christ, so that you may be overjoyed when his glory is revealed.
(1 PETER 4:12-13)

No one should regard his own suffering and distress as so horrible, as if it were new and had never happened to anyone before. It may well be new to you and you may not have experienced it before, but look around you at all the Christians in our beloved church from the beginning to this hour, planted in the world to run the devil's gauntlet and unceasingly winnowed and fanned like wheat. For where God through his Word and faith has gathered together a Church, the devil cannot be at peace, and where he cannot achieve her destruction through sectarianism he strikes at her with persecution and violence, so that we must risk our body and life in the faith, and all we have.

Martin Luther

23.7

Week Twenty-Four

THE HUMILITY OF SUFFERING

For we do not have a high priest who is unable to sympathize with our weaknesses, but we have one who has been tempted in every way, just as we are—yet was without sin.

(HEBREWS 4:15)

24.0

Christ transforms our suffering

Because he himself suffered when he was
tempted, he is able to help those
who are being tempted.
(HEBREWS 2:18)

How wonderful it is, is it not, that literally only Christianity has taught us the true peace and function of suffering. The Stoics tried the hopeless little game of denying its objective reality, or of declaring it a good in itself (which it never is), and the Pessimists attempted to revel in it, as a food to their melancholy, and as something that can no more be transformed than it can be avoided or explained. But Christ came, and he did not really explain it; he did far more; he met it, willed it, transformed it, and he taught us how to do all this, or rather he himself does it within us, if we do not hinder the all-healing hands.

Baron Friedrich von Hügel

24.1

The spirit of love makes suffering easy

Then Christ would have had to suffer many times since the creation of the world. But now he has appeared once for all at the end of the ages to do away with sin by the sacrifice of himself.
(HEBREWS 9:26)

Jesus Christ said to all Christians without exception, "Let him who would be my disciple carry his cross, and follow me." The broad way leads to perdition. We must follow the narrow way which few enter. . . . We must be born again, renounce ourselves, hate ourselves, become a child, be poor in spirit, weep to be comforted, and not be of the world, which is cursed because of its scandals. These truths frighten many people, and this is because they only know what religion exacts, without knowing what [Christ] offers, and they ignore the spirit of love which makes everything easy. They do not know that it leads to the highest perfection, by a feeling of peace and love which sweetens all the struggle.

Fénelon

No joy like the fellowship
of his suffering

For it has been granted to you on behalf
of Christ not only to believe on him,
but also to suffer for him.
(PHILIPPIANS 1:29)

Paradox of Christianity which no man can explain—
there is no joy like the fellowship of his suffering!
What is the sense of sin that causes you pain, dear
child of God? It is the outcome of purity. The
measure of purity is the measure of suffering in the
presence of sin. In the infinite mystery of pain there
is the deeper heart and core of holy joy. What is that
suffering of your heart in the presence of misunder-
standing of God? It is born of your perfect satisfaction in God. Why are you angry when that man libels
God? Because you know him. Your hot pain and
great sorrow come out of the quiet rest of intimate
knowledge. What is that pity for the sinner that
throbs through your soul, fills your eyes, breaks your
heart? It is the outcome of the love of God shed
abroad in your heart.

G. Campbell Morgan

24.3

In the fires of suffering God purifies his saints

How is it to your credit if you receive a beating for doing wrong and endure it? But if you suffer for doing good and you endure it, this is commendable before God.
(1 PETER 2:20)

It is in the fires of suffering that God purifies his saints and brings them to the highest things. It is in the furnace their faith is tested, their patience is tried, and they are developed in all those rich virtues which make up Christian character. It is while they are passing through deep waters that he shows how close he can come in his praying, believing saints. It takes faith of a high order and a Christian experience far above the average religion of this day, to count it joy when we are called to pass through tribulation. God's highest aim in dealing with his people is in developing Christian character. He is after begetting in us those rich virtues which belong to our Lord Jesus Christ. He is seeking to make us like himself.

E. M. Bounds

We never suffer except
for our good

I am the true vine, and my Father is the
gardener. He cuts off every branch in me
that bears no fruit, while every branch that
does bear fruit he prunes so that
it will be even more fruitful.
(JOHN 15:1-2)

God, who seems so stern to souls, never makes them suffer anything for the pleasure of making them suffer. He only plunges them into suffering to purify them. The rigor of the operation comes from the illness which must be done away with. No incision would be necessary if all were well. . . . The hand of God hurts as little as it can. Judge how deep and poisonous are our wounds, since God spares so much, and nevertheless makes us so violently suffer. Even when he never makes us suffer except for our healing, he does not take away one of his gifts without returning it a hundredfold.

Fénelon

Satan contrives to hinder our prayers

Do not deprive each other except by mutual consent and for a time, so that you may devote yourselves to prayer. Then come together again so that Satan will not tempt you because of your lack of self-control.

(1 CORINTHIANS 7:5)

Often I have wondered that I did not feel the temptations of Satan more frequently and plainly. But now I discover his plan. For a long time, indeed for years, I can see that he has contrived very many days to prevent my praying to any purpose. His temptations to me lie in the direction of putting half-lawful literature or literary work before me, which I am led on to read at once, without having first of all fully met with God. In short, he succeeds in reversing in my case, "Seek *first* the kingdom of God." Lord, give me power to resist. Lord, from this day give me many victories where formerly I fell under him.

Andrew A. Bonar

24.6

Suffering is a holy thing

So then, those who suffer according to God's will should commit themselves to their faithful Creator and continue to do good.
(1 PETER 4:19)

The suffering of Christians is nobler and finer than the suffering of all other people, for since Christ plunged himself into suffering he thereby sanctified the suffering of all his Christians. Now, through the sufferings of Christ the sufferings of all his saints are made into a holy thing because they are anointed with the sufferings of Christ. And this is why we must receive all suffering as a holy thing, for it truly is a holy thing.

Martin Luther

BE ENCOURAGED KNOWING HE LOVES YOU

As a young man marries a maiden, so will your sons marry you; as a bridegroom rejoices over his bride, so will your God rejoice over you.

(ISAIAH 62:5)

Be absolutely certain—
God loves you

As for man, his days are like grass,
he flourishes like a flower of the field;
the wind blows over it and it is gone,
and its place remembers it no more.
But from everlasting to everlasting the
LORD's *love is with those who fear him, and*
his righteousness with their children's children.
(PSALM 103:15-17)

Be absolutely certain that our Lord loves you, devotedly and individually: loves you just as you are. How often that conviction is lacking even in those souls who are most devoted to God! They make repeated efforts to love him, they experience the joy of loving, and yet how little they know, how little they realize, that God loves them incomparably more than they will ever know how to love him. Think only of this and say to yourself, "I am loved by God more than I can either conceive or understand." Let this fill all your soul and all your prayers and never leave you.

Henri de Tourville

25.1

The undistracted love of God

The LORD detests the way of the wicked
but he loves those who pursue righteousness.
(PROVERBS 15:9)

Involuntary distractions . . . do not disturb love at all, since it exists in the will, and the will never has distractions when it does not want to have them. . . . While the outer senses of the bride are slumbering, her heart watches, her love does not relax. A tender father does not always think distinctly of his son. A thousand objects take away his imagination and his mind. But these distractions never interrupt the paternal love. Whenever his son returns to his mind, he loves him, and he feels in the depths of his heart that he has not stopped loving him for a single moment, although he has stopped thinking of him. Such should be our love for our heavenly Father, a simple love without suspicion and without uneasiness.

Fénelon

25.2

The infinite God loves infinitely

*May our Lord Jesus Christ himself and God
our Father, who loved us and by his grace gave
us eternal encouragement and good hope,
encourage your hearts and strengthen you
in every good deed and word.*
(2 THESSALONIANS 2:16-17)

How much greater his love was, by so much the
greater may his sorrow be at the loss of his object: and
by so much the greater his desire also of its restora-
tion. His love therefore being infinite, may do infinite
things for an object infinitely valued. Being infinite in
wisdom, it is able also to devise a way inscrutable to
us, whereby to sever the sin from the sinner: and to
satisfy its righteousness in punishing the transgres-
sion, yet satisfy itself in saving the transgressor. . . .
But then it doth this at an infinite expense, wherein
also it is more delighted, and especially magnified, for
it giveth another equally dear unto itself to suffer in
its stead. And thus we come again by the works of
God to our Lord Jesus Christ.

Thomas Traherne

We are destined for great blessing

He will love you and bless you and increase your numbers. He will bless the fruit of your womb, the crops of your land . . . in the land that he swore to your forefathers to give you.
(DEUTERONOMY 7:13)

The blessings [God] bestows are all connected with his, "Come to me," and are to be enjoyed only in close fellowship with himself. You either did not fully understand, or did not rightly remember, that the call meant, "Come to *me* and stay with *me.*" And yet this was . . . his object and purpose when first he called you to himself. . . . He had destined you to something better than a short-lived blessedness, to be enjoyed only in times of special earnestness and prayer, and then to pass away. . . . He has prepared for you an abiding dwelling with himself, where your whole life and every moment of it might be spent, where the work of your daily life might be done, and where all the while you might be enjoying unbroken communion with him.

Andrew Murray

25.4

Hope in God

The LORD gives sight to the blind,
the LORD lifts up those who are bowed down,
the LORD loves the righteous.
(PSALM 146:8)

Teach us, O Lord to hope in thy name, which is the source and fount of all creation. Open the eyes of our hearts to know thee, who alone art Highest amid the highest, and ever abidest Holy amidst the holy. Thou dost bring down the haughtiness of the proud, and scatterest the devices of the people. Thou settest up the lowly on high, and the lofty thou dost cast down. Riches and poverty, death and life, are in thine hand; thou alone art the discerner of every spirit, and the God of man; thou art the aid of those in peril, the savior of them that despair, the creator and overseer of everything that hath breath. By thee the nations of the earth are increased; and from all mankind thou hast chosen out such as love thee through thy dear child Jesus Christ, by whom thou hast taught us and raised us to sanctification and honor.

Clement of Rome

25.5

Reconciled to God,
who loves me, even me

I will be a Father to you, and you will be my sons and daughters, says the Lord Almighty.
(2 CORINTHIANS 6:18)

The Scriptures teach us that God is love. But this is not enough to give me assurance of his favor so long as I read that he is angry with the wicked every day. Therefore, so long as I have a tormenting sense of guilt, I must be filled with painful forebodings till I have a positive and personal assurance that I am taken out of the class of the condemned, and am reconciled to God, who loves me, even me. This is the witness of the Spirit. . . . He is styled the Spirit of Adoption, because as such his chief message is to attest to the believer his pardon and sonship. When this glad evangel resounds within, love to God springs up responsive to his great love to me.

Daniel Steele

25.6

Our place in the family circle

God raised us up with Christ and seated us with him in the heavenly realms in Christ Jesus, in order that in the coming ages he might show the incomparable riches of his grace, expressed in his kindness to us in Christ Jesus.

(EPHESIANS 2:6-7)

Christ longs in an infinite desire and delight to communicate to us all he is and has, to make us partakers of his own nature and blessedness, to live in us and have us live in himself. And now, if Christ loves us with such an intense, such an infinite divine love, what is it that hinders it triumphing over every obstinance and getting full possession of us? The answer is simple. Even as the love of the Father to Christ, so his love to us is a divine mystery, too high for us to comprehend or attain to by any effort of our own. It is only the Holy Spirit who can shed abroad and reveal in its all-conquering power without intermission this wonderful love of God in Christ.

Andrew Murray

25.7

RESPONDING TO HIS LOVE

*I have made you known to them,
and will continue to make you known
in order that the love you have for me
may be in them and that I myself
may be in them.*

(JOHN 17:26)

26.0

Blessing for cursing

In bringing many sons to glory, it was fitting that God, for whom and through whom everything exists, should make the author of their salvation perfect through suffering.

(HEBREWS 2:10)

What manner of man is this, who in all his afflictions never once opened his mouth to utter a word of complaint or pleading, or of threatening or cursing against those accursed dogs, and last of all poured forth over his enemies a word of blessing such as hath not been heard from the beginning. What more gentle than this man, what more kind, O my soul, hast thou seen? Gaze on him, however, yet more intently, for he seemeth worthy both of great admiration and of most tender compassion. . . . Pour down your tears, mine eyes; melt, O my soul, with the fire of compassion at the sufferings of that Man of love, whom in the midst of such gentleness thou seest afflicted with so bitter griefs.

Anselm

26.1

Humility breaks the devil's snares

Humble yourselves, therefore,
under God's mighty hand,
that he may lift you up in due time.
(1 PETER 5:6)

When a lowly and loving man considers that God has served him so humbly, so lovingly, and so faithfully; and sees God so high, so mighty, and so noble, and man so poor, and so little, and so low; then there springs up within the humble heart a great awe and a great veneration for God. . . . And that is why a humble man thinks that his worship of God and his lowly service are always falling short. . . . He is humble in his devotions, both outwardly and inwardly before God and before all men, so that none is offended because of him. And so he overcomes and casts out pride, which is the source and origin of all other sins. By humility the snares of the devil, and of sin, and of the world are broken, and man is set in order and established in the very condition of virtue.

John of Ruysbroeck

26.2

Obliged to love God

However, as it is written: "No eye has seen, no ear has heard, no mind has conceived what God has prepared for those who love him."

(1 CORINTHIANS 2:9)

We must love God because he is our Creator. . . . We should love him also, because he has loved us, but with a tender love, like a father who pities his children, because he knows the mud and clay from which they have been made. He has sought us in our own ways, which are the ways of sin. He has run like a shepherd who tires himself to find his strayed lambs. He is not content to seek for us, but after he had found us, he took us and our weakness up himself. He was obedient even to death on the cross, and the measure of his obedience has been that of his love.

Fénelon

God is concerned with motives

From what you have, take an offering for the
LORD. Everyone who is willing is to bring to
the LORD an offering of gold, silver and
bronze. . . . All the Israelite men and women
who were willing brought to the LORD freewill
offerings for all the work the LORD through
Moses had commanded them to do.
(EXODUS 35:5, 29)

God does not so much seek our deeds as the motive
of love which makes us do them and the pliancy
which he exacts in our will. Men hardly judge our
actions except from without. God counts as nothing
everything in our actions which seems most brilliant
in the eyes of the world. What he wants is pure
intention. It is a will ready for everything and yielding in his hands.

Fénelon

Love: The real spring
of our life

*Delight yourself in the LORD
and he will give you the desires of your heart.*
(PSALM 37:4)

If we do a thing because we think it is our duty, we generally fail; that is the old law which makes slaves of us. The real spring of our life, and of our work in life, must be love—true, deep love—not love of this or that person, or for this or that reason, but deep human love, devotion of soul to soul, love of God realized when alone it can be—in love of those whom he loves. Everything else is weak, passes away; that love alone supports us, makes life tolerable, binds the present together with the past and future, and is, we may trust, imperishable.

Max Müller

Show no disloyalty
to the church

Let us not give up meeting together, as some
are in the habit of doing, but let us encourage
one another—and all the more
as you see the Day approaching.
(HEBREWS 10:25)

Let no one be under any illusion; a man who excludes himself from the sanctuary is depriving himself of the bread of God, for if the prayer of one or two individuals has such efficacy, how much more powerful is that of the bishop together with his church. Anyone who absents himself from the congregation convicts himself and becomes self-excommunicate. And since it is written that "God opposes the proud," let us take care to show no disloyalty to the bishop, so as to be loyal servants of God.

Ignatius of Antioch

Piety, simple and serene

God is spirit, and his worshipers
must worship in spirit and in truth.
(JOHN 4:24)

O how simple and serene piety can be! How likable, discreet, and sure in all its proceedings! One lives much as other people do, without affectation, without any show of austerity, in an easy and sociable way, but continually bound by all one's duties, but with an unrelenting renunciation of all which does not moment by moment enter into God's plan, in short with a pure vision of God to which one sacrifices the irregular impulses of human nature. This is the worship in spirit and in truth which Jesus Christ and his Father seek. All the rest is only a religion of ceremony, and the shadow rather than the truth of Christianity.

Fénelon

STRENGTHENED BY THE KNOWLEDGE OF HIS LOVE

God showed how much he loved us by sending his only Son into this wicked world to bring to us eternal life through his death.

(1 JOHN 4:9, TLB)

The communion: Reflection
of our love

*Then I heard everyone in heaven and earth,
and from the dead beneath the earth and in
the sea, exclaiming, "The blessing and the
honor and the glory and the power belong
to the one sitting on the throne,
and to the Lamb forever and ever."*

(REVELATION 5:13, TLB)

The most moving of all the reflections [Christian
history] brings is . . . the thought . . . of innumerable
millions of . . . faithful men and women. . . . Each of
them worshipped . . . and found their thoughts wandering and tried again, and felt heavy and unrespon-
sive. . . . There is a little ill-spelled, ill-carved rustic
epitaph of the fourth century from Asia minor:
"Here sleeps the blessed Chione, who has found
Jerusalem, for she prayed much.". . . What did the
Eucharist in her village church every week for a
lifetime mean to the millions like her then, and every
year since? The sheer stupendous quantity of the love
of God which this ever repeated action has drawn
from the obscure Christian multitudes . . . is in itself
an overwhelming thought.

Gregory Dix

27.1

The undisturbed kingdom
of God within

For Jehovah is my refuge! I choose the God above all gods to shelter me. How then can evil overtake me or any plague come near? For he orders his angels to protect you wherever you go. They will steady you with their hands to keep you from stumbling against the rocks on the trail. You can safely meet a lion or step on poisonous snakes, yes, even trample them beneath your feet! For the Lord says, "Because he loves me, I will rescue him; I will make him great because he trusts in my name."

(PSALM 91:9-14, TLB)

It does not take much time to love God, in order to renew ourselves in his presence, to raise our heart to him or to worship him in the depths of our heart, to offer him what we do and what we suffer. This is the true kingdom of God within us, which nothing can disturb.

Fénelon

27.2

Love that relates us to God

In this act we see what real love is: it is not our love for God, but his love for us when he sent his Son to satisfy God's anger against our sins.
(1 JOHN 4:10, TLB)

We want very much to love God on condition that we do not lessen in anything that blind love of ourselves, which goes as far as idolatry, and which causes us, instead of relating ourselves to God as to one for whom we were made, to want on the contrary to relate God to ourselves, and not to seek him except as a last resort, so that he may help us and comfort us, when creatures fail us. In truth, is this loving God? Is it not rather irritating to him?

Fénelon

God's infinite desire
for our companionship

Yes, I will rejoice over them to do them good,
and I will assuredly plant them in this land,
with all My heart and with all My soul.
(JEREMIAH 32:41, NKJV)

There is always that danger in religion—the danger of regarding God as a servant rather than the one utterly to be served. Of course, we do not put it to ourselves in those terms; we speak of a God of love and comfort, and we sing praises to his adequacy to our need. . . . But we must not stop there. There is a stranger and more astonishing thought, which sounds blasphemous perhaps to those who have not been gripped and overwhelmed by it, or who have not fully apprehended what we see in Jesus that God is, and that is the thought of God's need of us, of God's infinite desire for our companionship. [Jesus asked,] "Could ye not watch with me one hour?" We need Jesus, but Jesus quite desperately needs us, and that is what we do not realize when we protest our allegiance to him.

Herbert Henry Farmer

27.4

A child's love, not a slave's service

I no longer call you slaves, for a master doesn't confide in his slaves; now you are my friends, proved by the fact that I have told you everything the Father told me.
(JOHN 15:15, TLB)

Salvation is not only connected with the stopping of evil. To that must be added the practice of good. The kingdom of heaven is too great a prize to be given to a slavish fear, which only abstains from evil because it does not dare to commit it. God wants children who love his kindness, and not slaves who only serve him for fear of his power. So we must love him, and, consequently, do what a true love inspires.

Fénelon

Find in God a sure and a satisfying portion

The Lord will give you an abundance of good things in the land, just as he promised: many children, many cattle, and abundant crops. . . . He will bless everything you do.
(DEUTERONOMY 28:11-12, TLB)

The man who believes in the peculiar doctrines will readily bow to the peculiar demands of Christianity. When he is told to love God supremely, this may startle another; but it will not startle him to whom God has been revealed in peace and in pardon and in the freeness of an offered reconciliation. When told to shut out the world from his heart, this may be impossible with him who has nothing to replace it—but not impossible with him who has found in God a sure and a satisfying portion. . . . Separate the demands from the doctrine, and you have either a system of righteousness that is impracticable or a barren orthodoxy. Bring the demand and the doctrine together—and the true disciple of Christ is able to do the one through the other strengthening him.

Thomas Chalmers

27.6

We can trust someone who suffered for us

*So you see, our love for him comes
as a result of his loving us first.*
(1 JOHN 4:19, TLB)

Could you and I pass this day through these heavens, and see what is now going on in the sanctuary above . . . could you see the Lord with the scars of his five deep wounds in the very midst of the throne . . . could you see the many angels round the throne . . . all singing, "Worthy is the Lamb that was slain," and were one of these angels to tell you, "This is he that undertook the cause of lost sinners; he undertook to be the second Adam—the man in their stead; and lo! there he is upon the throne of heaven; consider him—look long and earnestly upon his wounds—upon his glory, and tell me, do you think it would be safe to trust him? Do you think his sufferings and obedience will have been enough? Yes, yes, every soul exclaims, Lord it is enough!

Robert Murray McCheyne

CONVICTION FROM GOD

*The blood of goats and bulls and
the ashes of a heifer sprinkled on those
who are ceremonially unclean sanctify
them so that they are outwardly clean.
How much more, then, will the blood
of Christ, who through the eternal
Spirit offered himself unblemished
to God, cleanse our consciences from
acts that lead to death, so that
we may serve the living God!*

(HEBREWS 9:13-14)

28.0

The pure light of God

*So I strive always to keep my conscience
clear before God and man.*
(ACTS 24:16)

Little faults become great and monstrous in our eyes
as the pure light of God increases in us. The sun, as
it rises, shows us the size of objects that we could
only make out obscurely during the night. Many
other miseries, which you could never have expected
to find, emerge in a crowd from your heart. You will
find there all the weakness that you will need to lose
confidence in your strength and . . . to raze to the
ground the whole edifice of pride. Nothing marks so
much the solid advancement of a soul as this view of
his wretchedness without anxiety and without dis-
couragement.

Fénelon

Guard your conscience

*Such teachings come through hypocritical
liars, whose consciences have been
seared as with a hot iron.*
(1 TIMOTHY 4:2)

We should reverence our consciences and stand in awe of them, and have a great regard to their testimony and verdict. For conscience is a domestic judge, and kind of a familiar god; and therefore next to the supreme Majesty of heaven and earth, every man should be afraid to offend his own reason and conscience which, whenever we knowingly do amiss, will beat us with many stripes and handle us more severely than the greatest enemy we have in the world. . . . The most sensual man that ever was in the world never felt his heart touched with so delicious and lasting a pleasure as that which springs from a clear conscience and a mind fully satisfied with his own actions. This makes all calm and serene within, when there is nothing but clouds and darkness about him.

John Tillotson

28.2

Give heed to the inner voice

Let us draw near to God with a sincere heart in full assurance of faith, having our hearts sprinkled to cleanse us from a guilty conscience and having our bodies washed with pure water.

(HEBREWS 10:22)

Conscience is the guardian or monitor God has given you, to give warning when anything goes wrong. Up to the light you have, give heed to conscience. Ask God, by the teaching of his will, to give it more light. Seek the witness of conscience that you are acting up to that light. Conscience will become your encouragement and helper, and give you the confidence, both that your obedience is accepted, and that your prayer for ever-increasing knowledge of the will is heard.

Andrew Murray

28.3

Put the small things
to good use

"Well done, my good servant!"
his master replied. "Because you have been
trustworthy in a very small matter,
take charge of ten cities."
(LUKE 19:17)

It is with piety as it is with economy in temporal things. If we do not take care of the things near us, we ruin ourselves more in incidental expenses than in great extravagances. Whoever knows how to put the small things to good use, spiritual as well as temporal, accumulates great wealth. All the great things are only made by the accumulation of little things that we receive with care. He who loses nothing will soon grow rich.

Fénelon

Inner character, not the
outward bearing

*Your beauty should not come from outward
adornment, such as braided hair and the
wearing of gold jewelry and fine clothes.
Instead, it should be that of your inner self,
the unfading beauty of a gentle and quiet
spirit, which is of great worth in God's sight.*
(1 PETER 3:3-4)

It was the inner character, not the outward bearing,
of such men as Abraham, Job, David, Moses, and
others, who had such great influence with God in
the days of old. And today, it is not so much our
words as what we really are that weighs with God.
Conduct affects character, of course, and counts for
much in our praying. At the same time, character
affects conduct to a far greater extent, and has a
superior influence over prayer. Our inner life not
only gives color to our praying, but body, as well.
Bad living means bad praying and, in the end, no
praying at all. We pray feebly because we live feebly.

E. M. Bounds

Keep the unity of the Spirit

Be completely humble and gentle;
be patient, bearing with one another in love.
Make every effort to keep the unity of the
Spirit through the bond of peace.
There is one body and one Spirit—just as you
were called to one hope when you were called.
(EPHESIANS 4:2-4)

Solitary Christians are apt to be weak Christians, for in this sphere as in all others, "union is strength." If Christian people are not truly knit together, the cause of Christ may suffer, for through the severances caused by division the enemy can keep thrusting his darts which must be parried alone. That is why the apostle . . . urges believers earnestly to strive "to keep the unity of the Spirit in the bond of peace" (Ephesians 4:3). One of the greatest powers that Satan wields today is due to disunion among the genuine people of God. It is true alike of the Christian home, congregation, and denomination. . . . On the other hand, where the brethren are able to "dwell together in unity," there the Lord commands his blessing (Psalm 133:3).

W. H. Griffith Thomas

28.6

Avoid introspection

Rather, we have renounced secret and
shameful ways; we do not use deception,
nor do we distort the word of God.
On the contrary, by setting forth the truth
plainly we commend ourselves to every man's
conscience in the sight of God.
(2 CORINTHIANS 4:2)

Live in peace without constantly quibbling about the secret motives which can unconsciously slip into the heart. We should never finish if we wanted constantly to sound the bottom of our hearts; and in wanting to escape from self in the search for God, we should be too preoccupied with self in such frequent examinations. Let us go on in simplicity of heart, in the peace and the joy, which are the fruits of the Holy Spirit.

Fénelon

RELUCTANT TO SEE OURSELVES

When Simon Peter saw this, he fell at Jesus' knees and said, "Go away from me, Lord; I am a sinful man!"

(LUKE 5:8)

In the presence of the all-seeing God

"Woe to me!" I cried. "I am ruined! For I am a man of unclean lips, and I live among a people of unclean lips, and my eyes have seen the King, the LORD Almighty."
(ISAIAH 6:5)

There is hardly a man or woman in the world who has not got some corner of self into which he or she fears to venture with a light. The reasons for this may be various. . . . But do we think that God cannot enter there except by our unlocking the door? . . . We know how his eye rests upon us incessantly, and takes us all in, and searches us out, and as it were burns us up with his holy gaze. . . . Yet, for all this, to be straightforward with God is neither an easy nor a common grace. O with what unutterable faith must we believe in our own falsehood, when we can feel it to be anything like a shelter in the presence of the all-seeing God!

Frederick William Faber

Self-control: Keep thyself
in peace

Above all else, guard your heart,
for it is the wellspring of life.
(PROVERBS 4:23)

First keep thyself in peace and then shalt thou be able to pacify others. A peaceable man doth more good than he that is well learned. . . . He that is well in peace is not suspicious of any. But he that is discontented and troubled is tossed with divers suspicions; he is neither quiet himself or suffereth others to be quiet. . . . He considereth what others are bound to do, and neglecteth that which he is bound to himself. First therefore have a careful zeal over thyself, and then thou mayest justly show thyself zealous also of thy neighbor's good.

Thomas à Kempis

29.2

Self-discipline: Small things do matter

He who conceals his sins does not prosper, but whoever confesses and renounces them finds mercy.
(PROVERBS 28:13)

We have a habit of thinking that small things do not matter. We do not consider them of enough consequence. . . . "That's nothing," we say. Yes, it is nothing, but a nothing which is all for you; a nothing, which you care enough for to refuse it to God; a nothing which you scorn in words so that you may have an excuse to refuse it, but, at bottom, is as a nothing which you are keeping back from God, and which will be your undoing.

Fénelon

Self-knowledge: See your own behavior

Search me, O God, and know my heart;
test my thoughts. Point out anything you
find in me that makes you sad, and lead me
along the path of everlasting life.
(PSALM 139:23-24, TLB)

We are strangely ingenious in perpetually seeking our own interest, and what worldly souls do crudely and openly, people who want to live for God often do more subtly, with the help of some pretext, which, serving them as a screen, stops them from seeing the ugliness of their behavior.

Fénelon

Self-love: A veil
upon our hearts

In the last days it is going to be very difficult
to be a Christian. For people will love only
themselves and their money; they will be proud
and boastful, sneering at God,
disobedient to their parents,
ungrateful to them, and thoroughly bad.
(2 TIMOTHY 3:1-2, TLB)

There is something more serious than coldness of
heart. . . . What is it? What but the presence of a veil
in our hearts? A veil not taken away as the first veil
was. . . . It is woven of the fine threads of the self-life,
the hyphenated sins of the human spirit. . . . To be
specific, the self-sins are these: self-righteousness,
self-pity, self-confidence, self-sufficiency, self-admi-
ration, self-love, and a host of others like them. . . .
They are so much in evidence as actually, for many
people, to become identified with the gospel. . . .
They appear these days to be a requisite for popular-
ity in some sections of the visible church. Promoting
self under the guise of promoting Christ is currently
so common as to excite little notice.

A. W. Tozer

29.5

Danger in self-examination

To the pure, all things are pure, but to those
who are corrupted and do not believe,
nothing is pure. In fact, both their minds
and consciences are corrupted.
(TITUS 1:15)

There is a danger . . . in self-examination, of de-
pending on the diligence of our own scrutiny rather
than on God for the discovery and knowledge of our
sins. This examination should be peaceful and tran-
quil. When we examine ourselves with effort, we can
easily be deceived and betrayed because self-love can
lead us to error. . . . Abandon yourself, then, in
examination as well as confession, to God. When
you are accustomed to this type of surrender, you
will find that as soon as a fault is committed God will
rebuke it through an inward burning. He allows no
evil to be concealed in the lives of his children. The
only way to deal with this is to turn simply to God
and bear the pain and correction he inflicts.

Jeanne Guyon

29.6

Character: Living in
contemplation of immortality

All our days pass away under your wrath; we
finish our years with a moan. The length of
our days is seventy years—or eighty, if we have
the strength; yet their span is but trouble and
sorrow, for they quickly pass, and we fly
away. . . . Teach us to number our days aright,
that we may gain a heart of wisdom.
(PSALM 90:9-10, 12)

There is a tendency in the masses always to think—
not what is true, but—what is respectable, correct,
orthodox; we ask is that authorized? It comes partly
from cowardice, partly from indolence; from habit;
from imitation; from the uncertainty and darkness of
all moral truth, and the dread of timid minds to
plunge into the investigation of them. Now, truth
known and believed respecting God and man, frees
from this, by warning of individual responsibility.
Fear enslaves; courage liberates—and that always.
Whatever man fears, that brings him into bondage. . . . From such fear Christ frees and through the
power of the truths I have spoken of.

Frederick W. Robertson

29.7

WHO WE ARE BEFORE GOD

*Consequently, you are no longer
foreigners and aliens, but fellow
citizens with God's people and members
of God's household, built on the
foundation of the apostles and prophets,
with Christ Jesus himself as the chief
cornerstone. In him the whole building
is joined together and rises to become a
holy temple in the Lord. And in him
you too are being built together to
become a dwelling in which God lives
by his Spirit.*

(EPHESIANS 2:19-22)

Consider your own works

For it is by grace you have been saved,
through faith—and this not from yourselves,
it is the gift of God—not by works,
so that no one can boast.
(EPHESIANS 2:8-9)

We cannot trust too much to ourselves, but grace oftentimes is wanting to us, and understanding also. There is but little light in us, and that which we have we quickly lose by our negligence. Oftentimes too we do not perceive our own inward blindness, how great it is. We often do evil, and excuse it worse. We are sometimes moved with passion, and we think it to be zeal. We reprehend small things in others, and pass over greater matters in ourselves. We quickly enough feel and weigh what we suffer at the hands of others; but we mind not what others suffer from us. He that well and rightly considereth his own works will find little cause to judge hardly of another.

Thomas à Kempis

Trust God for help against ourselves

As a father has compassion on his children,
so the LORD has compassion on those
who fear him; for he knows how we are formed,
he remembers that we are dust.
(PSALM 103:13-14)

We are in the dark about ourselves. When we act, we are groping in the dark, and may meet with a fall any moment. . . . The management of our hearts is quite above us. Under these circumstances it becomes our comfort to look up to God. "Thou, God, seest me!" Such was the consolation of the forlorn Hagar in the wilderness. He knoweth whereof we are made, and he alone can uphold us. He sees with most appalling distinctness all our sins, all the windings and recesses of evil within us; yet it is our only comfort to know this, and to trust him for help against ourselves. To those who have a right notion of their weaknesses, the thought of their Almighty Sanctifier and Guide is continually present . . . to change and strengthen them in their warfare with sin and Satan.

John Henry Newman

30.2

Let the Spirit take his course

In the same way, the Spirit helps us in our weakness. We do not know what we ought to pray for, but the Spirit himself intercedes for us with groans that words cannot express.
(ROMANS 8:26)

I used to spend a great deal of time in prayer. . . . Sometimes I would pursue a wrong course . . . and attempt to examine myself according to the ideas of self-examination. . . . I would try to look into my own heart, in the sense of examining my feelings, and would turn my attention particularly to my motives, and the state of my mind. When I pursued this course I found invariably that the day would close without any perceptible advance being made. Afterwards I saw clearly why this was so. Turning my attention, as I did, from the Lord Jesus Christ, and looking into myself, examining my motives and feelings, my feelings all subsided, of course. But . . . whenever I let the Spirit take his course with me . . . I universally found it in the highest degree useful to me.

Charles G. Finney

30.3

Self-love: A reversal of God's design

Those who walk in pride he is able to humble.
(DANIEL 4:37)

Before God, monstrous crimes, committed by weakness, by passion or by ignorance, are less crimes than are the virtues which a soul full of itself practices in order to relate everything to its own excellence, as though it alone were divine. For that is the total reversal of God's whole design for creation. Let us cease then to judge virtues and vices by our own taste, which self-love has made depraved, and by our false standards of greatness. There is no one great except he who makes himself very small before the unique and supreme greatness. You become great by the turning of your heart, and by our habit of turning it. But God wants to abase you and to make you small in his hand. Let him do this.

Fénelon

Change the disposition which makes us act

So now we can obey God's laws if we follow after the Holy Spirit and no longer obey the old evil nature within us.
(ROMANS 8:4, TLB)

Most people, when they wish to be converted or reformed, expect to fill their lives with especially difficult and unusual acts, far more than to purify their intentions, and to mortify their natural inclinations in the most usual acts of their condition. In this they often badly deceive themselves. It would be much more valuable for them to change their actions less, and to change more rather the disposition which makes them act.

Fénelon

Personal integrity:
Our first business

*Surely you desire truth in the inner parts;
you teach me wisdom in the inmost place.*
(PSALM 51:6)

Foolish is the man . . . who would rid himself or his fellows of discomfort by setting the world right, by waging war on the evils around him, while he neglects that integral part of the world where lies his business, his first business—namely, his own character and conduct. There is no way of making three men right but by making right each one of the three; but a cure in one man who repents and turns is a beginning of the cure of the whole human race. Rightness alone is cure. The return of the organism to its true self is its only possible ease. To free a man from suffering, he must be set right, put in health; and the health at the root of man's being, his rightness, is to be free from wrongness, that is, from sin. A man is right when there is no wrong in him. The wrong, the evil is in him, he must be set free from it.

George Macdonald

Unity: One body dependent on one head

We will lovingly follow the truth at all times—speaking truly, dealing truly, living truly—and so become more and more in every way like Christ who is the Head of his body, the Church.
(EPHESIANS 4:15, TLB)

All the elect are so united in Christ that as they are dependent on one Head, they also grow together into one body, being joined and knit together as are the limbs of a body. . . . They have been called not only into the same inheritance of eternal life but also to participate in one God and Christ. Although the melancholy desolation which confronts us on every side may cry that no remnant of the church is left, let us know that Christ's death is fruitful, and that God miraculously keeps his church as in hiding places. So it was said to Elijah, "I have kept for myself seven thousand men who have not bowed the knee before Baal" (1 Kings 19:18).

John Calvin

30.7

SPARE NOT SELF

*Do not offer the parts of your body to
sin, as instruments of wickedness, but
rather offer yourselves to God, as those
who have been brought from death to
life; and offer the parts of your body to
him as instruments of righteousness.
For sin shall not be your master,
because you are not under law,
but under grace.*

(ROMANS 6:13-14)

Risk nothing,
accomplish nothing

Then Jesus said to his disciples, "If anyone would come after me, he must deny himself and take up his cross and follow me. For whoever wants to save his life will lose it, but whoever loses his life for me will find it."
(MATTHEW 16:24-25)

Since I have been in the ministry, I have been pressed, I cannot say how many times, to spare myself and take more rest, and take more care of myself. But Jesus Christ laid down his life, and I can afford, if necessary, to lay down mine. It is not the point how long anyone lives, but what he does. If a man is endeavoring to spare his own health, and to make that a primary object, setting it before his duty—he is not doing very much. . . . To preserve one's life is a duty, when it can be done consistently with other and more important duties. But it is often our duty to sacrifice life, or at least, to risk it; and the man who cannot do this will never accomplish very great things. The work must be done, come life or come death.

Charles G. Finney

31.1

Gain all by losing everything

The man who loves his life will lose it,
while the man who hates his life in this world
will keep it for eternal life.
(JOHN 12:25)

Let no one imagine that he will lose anything of human dignity by this voluntary sell-out of his all to his God. He does not by this degrade himself as a man; rather he finds his right place of high honor as one made in the image of his Creator. His deep disgrace lay in his moral derangement, his unnatural usurpation of the place of God. His honor will be proved by restoring again that stolen throne. In exalting God over all he finds his own highest honor upheld.

A. W. Tozer

Keep yourself from wrongdoing

I can do anything I want to if Christ has not said no, but some of these things aren't good for me. Even if I am allowed to do them, I'll refuse to if I think they might get such a grip on me that I can't easily stop when I want to.
(1 CORINTHIANS 6:12, TLB)

Let us keep ourselves with the utmost strictness from any kind of wrongdoing; otherwise wrongdoing will get the better of us. Let there be hatred in us for the errors of this world, so that there may be love for us in the world to come. We must not give such rein to our natural instincts that we feel ourselves free to mix at will with rogues and sinners, or we shall only grow to resemble them.

Barnabas

31.3

He is merciful toward our unavoidable weaknesses

When we were overwhelmed by sins,
you forgave our transgressions.
(PSALM 65:3)

Although the goodness of God, and his rich mercies in Christ Jesus, are a sufficient assurance to us, that he will be merciful to our unavoidable weaknesses and infirmities, that is, to such failings as are the effects of ignorance or surprise; yet we have no reason to expect the same mercy toward those sins which we have lived in, through a want of intention to avoid them. . . . If you are as forward in the Christian life as your best endeavors can make you, then you may justly hope that your imperfections will not be laid to your charge. But if your defects in piety, humility, and charity are owing to your negligence and want of sincere intention to be as eminent as you can in these virtues, then you leave yourself as much without excuse as he that lives in . . . sin through the sincere intention to depart from it.

William Law

31.4

He will hold us accountable

They will have to give account to him who is
ready to judge the living and the dead.
(1 PETER 4:5)

Every hour is loaded with duties which God has
allotted to it with his own hand, and for which he
will hold us accountable; because from the first
seconds of our existence until the last moment of
our life, God has not intended to leave us any empty
time, nor any which might be said to be left to our
discretion, or for us to lose. The important thing is
to know what he wants us to do with it.

Fénelon

31.5

Consecration: A principle
of conduct

Don't copy the behavior and customs of this world,
but be a new and different person with a fresh
newness in all you do and think. Then you
will learn from your own experience
how his ways will really satisfy you.
(ROMANS 12:2, TLB)

We want a principle of conduct, a truth which will satisfy reason, a flow of inward life. We want all these, each for its own sake, and each for the sake of the others; yet for the sake of one we are constantly driven to sacrifice the rest. There is but one perfect unity and that is in the heavens: yet it came down from the heavens that we might be raised into fellowship with it. Daily taking up the cross and following Jesus as Lord, daily turning and becoming as little children in the sonship of the Heavenly Father, are the means by which it is attained. So with all our inconsistencies and weaknesses and sins we are kept in the one Way, the one Truth, and the one Life; and each step that we take brings us nearer to the one Father above.

F. J. A. Hort

31.6

Be willing to follow
him to Calvary

Those who belong to Christ Jesus
have crucified the sinful nature
with its passions and desires.
(GALATIANS 5:24)

Those who are devoted to God only insofar as they feel the joy and consolation of his presence, are like the people who followed Jesus, not for his teaching, but for the miraculously multiplied bread. They say, like Peter, "Lord it is good for us to be here. Let us make three tabernacles here." But they do not know what they are saying. After being intoxicated by the rapture of Tabor, they misunderstand the Son of God and refuse to follow him to Calvary. Not only do they seek the joys, but they want still more illumination. The mind is curious to see, while the heart wants to be stirred by sweet and flattering feelings. Is that dying to self?

Fénelon

UNDERSTANDING DISCIPLINE

But we ought always to thank God for you, brothers loved by the Lord, because from the beginning God chose you to be saved through the sanctifying work of the Spirit and through belief in the truth. He called you to this through our gospel, that you might share in the glory of our Lord Jesus Christ.

(2 THESSALONIANS 2:13-14)

Consecration of the entire person

May God himself, the God of peace, sanctify you through and through. May your whole spirit, soul and body be kept blameless at the coming of our Lord Jesus Christ.

(1 THESSALONIANS 5:23)

Our Lord Jesus Christ was preeminent in praying because he was preeminent in saintliness. An entire dedication to God, a full surrender, which carries with it the whole being in a flame of holy consecration—all this gives wings to faith and energy to prayer. It opens the door to the throne of grace and brings strong influence to bear on Almighty God. The "lifting up of holy hands" is essential to Christlike praying. It is not, however, a holiness that only dedicates a closet to God, which sets apart merely an hour to him, but a consecration which takes hold of the entire man, which dedicates the whole life to God.

E. M. Bounds

32.1

Never cease to detest evil

In him you were also circumcised, in the putting off of the sinful nature, not with a circumcision done by the hands of men but with the circumcision done by Christ.

(COLOSSIANS 2:11)

Never hesitate to give; and when you are giving, do it without grumbling; you will soon find out Who can be generous with his rewards. Keep the traditions you have received, without making any additions or deductions of your own. Never cease to detest evil. Make your decisions fairly and uprightly. Do nothing to encourage dissensions. Bring the disputants together, and compose their quarrel. And make confession of your own faults; you are not to come to prayer with a bad conscience. That is the Way of Light.

Barnabas

Be intent on pleasing God

It is God's will that you should be sanctified:
that you should avoid sexual immorality; that
each of you should learn to control his own
body in a way that is holy and honorable.
(1 THESSALONIANS 4:3-4)

You see two persons; one is regular in public and
private prayer, the other is not. Now the reason of
this difference is not . . . that one has strength and
power to observe prayer and the other has not, but
the reason is . . . that one intends to please God. . . .
The case is the same, in the right or wrong use of our
time and money. You see one person throwing away
his time in sleep and idleness and his money in the
most vain and unreasonable expenses. You see another careful of every day, dividing his hours by rules
of reason and religion, and spending his money in
works of charity. The difference is not that one has
strength and power to do this and the other has not.
It is because one intends to please God in the right
use of all his time and money and the other has no
intention about it.

William Law

32.3

Recognize the symptoms of the possession malady

If anyone has material possessions and sees his brother in need but has no pity on him, how can the love of God be in him?
(1 JOHN 3:17)

Our gifts and talents should . . . be turned over to [God.] They should be recognized for what they are, God's loan to us, and should never be considered in any sense our own. We have no more right to claim credit for special abilities than for blue eyes or strong muscles, "For who maketh thee to differ from another? And what hast thou that thou didst not receive?" The Christian who is alive enough to know himself even slightly will recognize the symptoms of this possession malady, and will grieve to find them in his own heart. If the longing after God is strong enough within him he will want to do something about the matter.

A. W. Tozer

Be thankful for every minute

Do not be anxious about anything, but in everything, by prayer and petition, with thanksgiving, present your requests to God.
(PHILIPPIANS 4:6)

How thankful we ought to be every minute of our existence to him who gives us all richly to enjoy! How little one has deserved this happy life, much less than many poor sufferers to whom life is a burden and a hard and bitter trial! But then, how much greater the claims on us; how much more sacred the duty never to trifle, never to waste time and power, but to live in all things, small and great, to the glory and praise of God, to have God always present with us, and to be ready to follow his voice and his voice only! Has our prosperity taught us to meet adversity when it comes? I often tremble, but then I commit all to God, and I say, "Have mercy upon me, miserable sinner."

Max Müller

All things are his

"The silver is mine and the gold is mine,"
declares the LORD Almighty.
(HAGGAI 2:8)

All his life, Jesus was among his Father's things, either in heaven or in the world. . . . he claimed none of them as his own, would not have had one of them his except through his Father. Did he ever say, "This is mine, not yours"? Did he not say, "All things are mine, therefore they are yours"? That the things were his Father's made them precious things to him. Oh, for his liberty among the things of the Father! Only by knowing them the things of our Father can we escape enslaving ourselves to them.

George Macdonald

How little we deserve!

For the LORD God is a sun and shield; the LORD bestows favor and honor; no good thing does he withhold from those whose walk is blameless. O LORD Almighty, blessed is the man who trusts in you.
(PSALM 84:11-12)

For disappointments that come not by our own folly, they are the trials or corrections of heaven: and it is our own fault if they prove not to our advantage. To repine at them does not mend the matter: it is only to grumble at our Creator. But to see the hand of God in them, with a humble submission to his will, is the way to turn our water into wine and engage the greatest love and mercy on our side. We must needs disorder ourselves if we look only at our losses. But if we consider how little we deserve what is left, our passion will cool, and our murmurs will turn into thankfulness. If our hairs fall not to the ground, less do we or our substance without God's providence. Nor can we fall below the arms of God, how low soever it be we fall.

William Penn

32.7

EVERY DAY A JOURNEY

So then, just as you received Christ Jesus as Lord, continue to live in him, rooted and built up in him, strengthened in the faith as you were taught, and overflowing with thankfulness.

(COLOSSIANS 2:6-7)

Following Christ every day

Since we live by the Spirit,
let us keep in step with the Spirit.
(GALATIANS 5:25)

If we are to follow Christ, it must be in our common
way of spending every day. Thus it is in all the virtues
and holy tempers of Christianity; they are not ours
unless they be the virtues and tempers of our ordinary life. So that Christianity is so far from leaving
us to live in the common ways of life, conforming to
the folly of customs, and gratifying the passions and
tempers which the spirit of the world delights in. . . .
If our common life is not a common course of
humility, self-denial, renunciation of the world, poverty of spirit, and heavenly affection, we do not live
the lives of Christians.

William Law

Live the same way everyday

Then he said to them all: "If anyone would come after me, he must deny himself and take up his cross daily and follow me."
(LUKE 9:23)

If some people fancy that they must be grave and solemn at church, but may be silly and frantic at home; that they must live by some rule on Sunday, but may spend other days by chance; that they must have some times of prayer, but may waste the rest of their time as they please . . . such people have not enough considered the nature of religion, or the true reasons of piety. For he that upon principles of reason can tell why it is good to be wise and heavenly-minded at church, can tell that it is always desirable to have the same tempers in all other places. He that truly knows why he should spend any time well knows that it is never allowable to throw any time away.

William Law

33.2

Follow godly examples

*Remember your leaders, who spoke the word of
God to you. Consider the outcome of their
way of life and imitate their faith.*
(HEBREWS 13:7)

When you would represent to your mind, how
Christians ought to live unto God, and in what
degrees of wisdom and holiness they ought to use
things of this life, you must not look at the world,
but you must look up to God, and the society of
Angels, and think what wisdom and holiness is fit to
prepare for such a state of glory. You must look at all
the highest precepts of the Gospel, you must examine yourself by the spirit of Christ, you must think
how the wisest men in the world have lived, you
must think how departed souls would live if they
were again to act the short part of human life; you
must think what degrees of wisdom and holiness you
wish for, when you are leaving the world.

William Law

Love God with all your heart

Love the LORD, all his saints!
The LORD preserves the faithful, but the proud
he pays back in full. Be strong and take heart,
all you who hope in the LORD.
(PSALM 31:23-24)

There are three things that are very sublime and very profitable, which he who has once acquired shall never rail.

The first is that thou bear willingly and gladly, for the love of Christ, every affliction that shall befall thee.

The second is that thou daily humble thyself in everything thou doest, and in everything thou seest.

The third is that thou love faithfully with all thy heart that invisible and supreme Good which thou canst not behold with thy bodily eyes.

Brother Giles

33.4

Best Christians found in
the worst of times

The LORD is a refuge for the oppressed, a stronghold in times of trouble. Those who know your name will trust in you, for you, LORD, have never forsaken those who seek you.
(PSALM 9:9-10)

I have often thought that the best Christians are found in the worst of times: and I have thought again, that one reason why we are no better, is because God purges us no more. I know these things are against the grain of the flesh, but they are not against the graces of the Spirit. Noah and Lot, who so holy as they, in the day of their affliction? Noah and Lot, who so idle as they in the day of their prosperity? I might have put in David too, who, while he was afflicted, had ways of serving God that were special; but when he was enlarged, he had ways that were not so good. . . . Wherefore for a conclusion, as we are to receive with meekness the engrafted word of God, so also we are with patience to bear what God, by man, shall lay upon us.

John Bunyan

33.5

Every inordinate its
own punishment

*As I have observed, those who plow evil
and those who sow trouble reap it.*
(JOB 4:8)

But you, by whom the very hairs of our head are numbered, did use for my good the error of all who urged me to learn; and my own, who would not learn. You used for my punishment—a fit penalty for one, so small a boy and so great a sinner. So by those who did not well, you did well for me; and by my own sin you did justly punish me. For you have commanded, and so it is, that every inordinate affection should be its own punishment.

Augustine of Hippo

His designs toward you:
Sanctification

May I never boast except in the cross of our Lord Jesus Christ, through which the world has been crucified to me, and I to the world.
(GALATIANS 6:14)

I am fully persuaded of his designs toward you, as well for the sanctification of others, as for your own sanctification. Let me assure you, this is not attained, save through pain, weariness and labor; and it will be reached by a path that will wonderfully disappoint your expectations. Nevertheless, if you are fully convinced that it is on the nothingness in man that God establishes his greatest works, you will be in part guarded against disappointment or surprise. He destroys that he might build; for when he is about to rear his sacred temple in us, he first totally razes that vain and pompous edifice, which human art and power had erected, and from its horrible ruins a new structure is formed by his power only.

Jeanne Guyon

Week Thirty-Four

THE JOURNEY HEAVENWARD

*Those who are wise will shine like the
brightness of the heavens, and those who
lead many to righteousness, like the
stars for ever and ever.*

(DANIEL 12:3)

34.0

Long-sighted people

For here we do not have an enduring city, but
we are looking for the city that is to come.
(HEBREWS 13:14)

Abraham was what you might call a long-sighted man; he had his eyes set on the city which had foundations—"whose Builder and Maker is God." But Lot was a short-sighted man; and there are many people in the church who are very short-sighted; they only see things right around them and they think good. . . . Paul was another of those long-sighted men; he had been caught up and seen things unlawful for him to utter; things grand and glorious. I tell you, when the Spirit of God is on us the world looks very empty; the world has a very small hold upon us, and we . . . will just let go the things of time and lay hold of things eternal. This is the church's need today. . . . Oh! that the Spirit of fire may come down and burn everything in us that is contrary to God's blessed Word and will.

Dwight L. Moody

Think about heaven

And I confer on you a kingdom,
just as my Father conferred one on me,
so that you may eat and drink at my table
in my kingdom and sit on thrones,
judging the twelve tribes of Israel.
(LUKE 22:29-30)

Another advantage arising from frequently thinking about heaven is that we will be less likely to have a wrong love for earthly things (Luke 14:26). I am . . . thinking of those who would claim to be interested in spiritual things, who gain their wealth in lawful and honest ways and who live in a moderate way. There is nothing wrong in all that they do, yet they sometimes ask to be excused from helping charitable causes . . . or from taking on church duties. . . . What is expected of them would not, in fact, deprive their families of necessary support, nor damage their businesses! But by being satisfied with excuses they demonstrate their priority is *this* life, not the next.

John Owen

Faith grows stronger thinking about heaven

I pray also that the eyes of your heart may be enlightened in order that you may know the hope to which he has called you, the riches of his glorious inheritance in the saints.

(EPHESIANS 1:18)

Several advantages are to be expected from regularly thinking about heaven. In the same way as when one looks at a bright light and the image of that brightness afterwards blinds one to other sights for a while, so whoever meditates on heavenly glories will find desire for earthly things lessened. . . . Faith will grow stronger by thoughts about heaven. The more that believers think about heaven, the more they will look forward to being there. Those who do not think of heaven frequently, do not think of it sincerely. As a result of strong faith, believers have a bright hope. . . . The reason why believers sometimes lack hope is because they do not think often enough about the things hoped for.

John Owen

34.3

Happiness is a by-product

*Blessed are you when people insult you,
persecute you and falsely say all kinds of evil
against you because of me. Rejoice and be
glad, because great is your reward in heaven,
for in the same way they persecuted the
prophets who were before you.*
(MATTHEW 5:11-12)

Many things that we most desire can be obtained only if we do not aim directly at them. . . . Happiness is one of them. . . . You cannot read the Gospels without seeing that Jesus did not tell men how to be good. . . . He told them how to be happy. The beatitudes . . . suggest that happiness is a by-product of . . . things such as . . . humility and mercy and purity of heart and being persecuted for righteousness' sake. These sound like paradoxes, for it is by no means self-evident that the meek shall inherit the earth or that it is better to give than to receive. . . . We err in treating these . . . as paradoxes. It would be nearer the truth to say that life itself is a paradox and that the sayings of Jesus are simply a recognition of that fact.

T. M. Taylor

34.4

The source of all satisfaction

*And I—in righteousness I will see your face;
when I awake, I will be satisfied
with seeing your likeness.*
(PSALM 17:15)

When the Lord divided Canaan among the tribes of Israel, Levi received no share of the land. God said to him simply, "I am thy part and thine inheritance," and by those words made him richer than all his brethren, richer than all the kings and rajas who have ever lived in the world. And there is a spiritual principle here, a principle still valid for every priest of the Most High God. The man who has God for his treasure has all things in One. Many ordinary treasures may be denied him, or if he is allowed to have them, the enjoyment of them will be so tempered that they will never be necessary to his happiness. Or if he must see them go, one by one, he will scarcely feel a sense of loss, for having the Source of all things he has in One all satisfaction, all pleasure, all delight.

A. W. Tozer

34.5

That which truly satisfies

We have heard of your faith in Christ Jesus
and of the love you have for all the saints—
the faith and love that spring from the hope
that is stored up for you in heaven
and that you have already heard about
in the word of truth, the gospel.
(COLOSSIANS 1:4-5)

They waste their energies in unrewarding efforts; yet they accomplish nothing, for, setting their affections on created things, they try them all in turn before they dream of trying God from whom all things proceed. Suppose they did get everything they wanted, what would happen then? One treasure after another would fail to satisfy, and then the only object of desire left would be the cause of all. It is our nature's law that makes a man set higher value on the things he has not got than upon those he has, so that he loathes his actual possessions for longings for the things that are not his. And this same law, when all things else in earth and heaven have failed, drives him at last to God, the Lord of all, whom hitherto alone he has not had.

Bernard of Clairvaux

34.6

Associate with the good and gentle

Share with God's people who are in need.
Practice hospitality. Bless those who persecute
you; bless and do not curse. Rejoice with those
who rejoice; mourn with those who mourn.
(ROMANS 12:13-15)

Thou knowest well how to excuse and color thine own deeds, but thou art not willing to receive the excuses of others. It were more just that thou shouldest accuse thyself and excuse thy brother. . . . It is no great matter to associate with the good and gentle; for this is naturally pleasing to all, and everyone willingly enjoyeth peace and loveth those best that agree with him. But to be able to live peaceably with hard and perverse persons, or with the disorderly or with such as go contrary to us, is a great grace and a most commendable and manly thing.

Thomas à Kempis

THE WALK OF FAITH

These were all commended for their faith, yet none of them received what had been promised. God had planned something better for us so that only together with us would they be made perfect.

(HEBREWS 11:39-40)

God's giants have been weak men

*By faith Abraham, even though he was past
age—and Sarah herself was barren—was
enabled to become a father because he
considered him faithful
who had made the promise.*
(HEBREWS 11:11)

All God's giants have been weak men, who did great
things for God because they reckoned on God being
with them. See the cases of David, of Jonathan, and
his armor-bearer, of Asa, Jehoshaphat, and many
others. Oh! beloved friends, if there is a living God,
faithful and true, let us hold his faithfulness. Holding his faithfulness, we may face, with calm and
sober but confident assurance of victory, every difficulty and danger. We may count on grace for the
work, on pecuniary aid, on needful facilities, and on
ultimate success. Let us not give him a partial trust,
but daily, hourly, serve him, "holding God's faithfulness."

J. Hudson Taylor

35.1

God's power preserves
our spirit

*My message and my preaching were not with
wise and persuasive words, but with a
demonstration of the Spirit's power, so that
your faith might not rest on men's wisdom,
but on God's power.*

(1 Corinthians 2:4)

Believers should often meditate on God's *power*.
They will never enjoy real peace of mind or comfort
of soul unless their minds are often occupied with
thoughts of the almighty power of God (Psalm
62:11). Failure to think about God's power will
result in believers being very troubled by things that
happen to them. They should also consider God's
promises made to the church, which are not yet
fulfilled, whenever they feel the evil in the world
endangers the church. Unless they are assured of
God's power, they may become very uncertain about
the future of the church. The thought of passing
through death may well frighten us, unless we trust
in God's power to preserve our spirits and ultimately
to resurrect our bodies. To die without fear requires
complete confidence in the almighty power of God.

John Owen

35.2

The faithfulness of the
Lord our Shepherd

*And pray that we may be delivered from
wicked and evil men, for not everyone has
faith. But the Lord is faithful, and he will
strengthen and protect you from the evil one.*

(2 THESSALONIANS 3:2-3)

Surely in a world like this, where every thing is
uncertain, where we are exposed to trials on every
hand, and know not but a single hour may bring
forth something painful, yea dreadful, to our natural
sensations, there can be no blessedness but so far as
we are thus enabled to entrust and resign all to the
direction and faithfulness of the Lord our Shepherd.
For want of more of this spirit multitudes of profess-
ing Christians perplex and wound themselves and
dishonor their high calling by continual anxieties,
alarms, and complaints. . . . But blessed is the man
who trusteth in the Lord and whose hope the Lord
is.

John Newton

35.3

Avoid a gloomy life

In all my prayers for all of you, I always pray with joy because of your partnership in the gospel from the first day until now, being confident of this, that he who began a good work in you will carry it on to completion until the day of Christ Jesus.

(PHILIPPIANS 1:4-6)

When pleasures are harmless in themselves, and when we take part in them because of the obligations of the state into which Providence has called us, then I believe that it is enough to take part in them with moderation, and in the sight of God. More severe, more constrained, less agreeable and disarming manners would only give a false idea of piety to the people of the world, who are already only too prejudiced against it, and who would think that a person can only serve God by a grim and gloomy life.

Fénelon

35.4

Know God, not know about God

Since then, no prophet has risen in Israel like
Moses, whom the LORD knew face to face,
who did all those miraculous signs and
wonders the LORD sent him to do in Egypt. . . .
For no one has ever shown the mighty power or
performed the awesome deeds that Moses did in
the sight of all Israel.
(DEUTERONOMY 34:10-12)

To believe that God is omnipotent . . . when that
belief is the mere admission of a dogma in theology
. . . will go but a little way toward strengthening you
in that faith which glorifies God. But let me again
remind you that the faith in question is believing
God; not believing something about God, but believing God. It is a personal dealing of God with you,
and of you with God. He and you come together; he
to speak, you to hear; he to promise, you to believe;
you to ask, he to give.

Robert S. Candlish

35.5

Trust Christ alone for salvation

Salvation is found in no one else,
for there is no other name under heaven
given to men by which we must be saved.
(ACTS 4:12)

In the evening I went very unwillingly to a society in Aldersgate Street, where one was reading Luther's preface to the Epistle to the Romans. About a quarter before nine, while he was describing the change which God works in the heart through faith in Christ, I felt my heart strangely warmed. I felt I did trust in Christ, Christ alone, for my salvation; and an assurance was given me that he had taken away my sins, even mine, and saved me from the law of sin and death. . . . But it was not long before the enemy suggested, "This cannot be faith; for where is thy joy?" Then was I taught that . . . as to the transports of joy . . . in those who have mourned deeply, God sometimes giveth, sometimes withholdeth them, according to the counsels of his own will.

John Wesley

35.6

Jesus seeing us, loves us

Who shall separate us from the love of Christ?
Shall trouble or hardship or persecution or
famine or nakedness or danger or sword? As it
is written: "For your sake we face death all day
long; we are considered as sheep to be
slaughtered." No, in all these things we are
more than conquerors through him who loved us.
(ROMANS 8:35-37)

Jesus did love a man who was able, sometimes, to be
reckless. He did not care for the rulers as a class, but
when one of them forgot his dignity, and ran after a
peasant teacher and fell on the road at his feet, we
read that "Jesus, seeing him, loved him." He did not
choose for his disciples discreet and futile persons,
but a man whose temper was not always under control, and whose tongue was rough when he was
roused, and another who might have been a saint,
but his life got twisted and he betrayed his Lord. He
saw a widow flinging into the treasury all that she
had, which no doubt was a very foolish action, but it
stirred his heart with gladness to see somebody ven-
turing herself simply upon God.

W. M. MacGregor
35.7

LEARNING TO BE A CHILD OF THE KINGDOM

But I tell you: Love your enemies and pray for those who persecute you, that you may be sons of your Father in heaven.

(MATTHEW 5:44)

The purpose of life:
Shaping character

And having chosen us, he called us to come to him; and when we came, he declared us "not guilty," filled us with Christ's goodness, gave us right standing with himself, and promised us his glory.
(ROMANS 8:29-30, TLB)

The great purpose of life—the shaping of character by truth—is to be sought in all the life. There are no wasted hours. It must begin in the life's morning and run on till the nightfall comes. . . . In the early life the channel through which truth enters for its work is obedient trust. Later it is individual conviction; but he mangles the life, and loses its symmetry and unity, who breaks off either half or dishonors either channel; who either thinks there can be no religion till the mind can understand its grounds, or tries to keep the mature mind under the power of traditional ideas of which it has received no personal conviction.

Phillips Brooks

36.1

Worship: Real devotion

The fruit of righteousness will be peace;
the effect of righteousness will be quietness
and confidence forever.
(ISAIAH 32:17)

Activity is not strength. Work is not zeal. Moving about is not devotion. Activity often is the unrecognized symptom of spiritual weakness. It may be hurtful to piety when made the substitute for real devotion in worship. The colt is much more active than its mother, but she is the wheel-horse of the team, pulling the load without noise or bluster or show. The child is more active than the father, who may be bearing the rule and burdens of an empire on his heart and shoulders. Enthusiasm is more active than faith, though it cannot remove mountains nor call into action any of the omnipotent forces which faith can command.

E. M. Bounds

Be a child

*Love your enemies, do good to them, and lend
to them without expecting to get anything
back. Then your reward will be great, and you
will be sons of the Most High, because he is
kind to the ungrateful and wicked.*
(LUKE 6:35)

Be free, joyful, simple, a child. But be a sturdy child, who fears nothing, who speaks out frankly, who lets himself be led, who is carried in the arms; in a word, one who knows nothing, can do nothing, can anticipate and change nothing, but who has a freedom and strength forbidden to the great. This childhood baffles the wise, and God himself speaks by the mouth of such children.

Fénelon

The joy of the Lord

This day is sacred to our LORD.
Do not grieve, for the joy of the LORD
is your strength.
(NEHEMIAH 8:10)

Do all God's children understand this, that holiness is just another name, the true name, that God gives for happiness; that it is, indeed, unutterable blessedness to know that God does make us holy, that our holiness is in Christ, that Christ's Holy Spirit is within us? There is nothing so attractive as joy: have believers understood that this is the joy of the Lord—to be holy? Or is not the idea of strain, and sacrifice, and sighing, of difficulty and distance, so prominent, that the thought of being holy has hardly ever made the heart glad? If it has been so, let it be so no longer.

Andrew Murray

Holiness and happiness,
joined in one

In the house of the wise are stores of choice food and oil, but a foolish man devours all he has. He who pursues righteousness and love finds life, prosperity and honor.
(PROVERBS 21:20-21)

Holiness and happiness, joined in one, are sometimes styled, in the inspired writings, "the kingdom of God" . . . because it is the immediate fruit of God's reigning in the soul. So soon as ever he takes unto himself his mighty power, and sets up his throne in our hearts, they are instantly filled with this "righteousness, and peace, and joy in the Holy Ghost" (Romans 14:17). It is called "the kingdom of heaven" because it is, in a degree, heaven opened in the soul. For whosoever they are that experience this, they can say before angels and men: "Everlasting life is won,/ Glory is on earth begun."

John Wesley

Seek after peace

Turn from evil and do good;
seek peace and pursue it.
(PSALM 34:14)

If you are a Christian indeed, you will have such a value and esteem for peace, as to endeavor to obtain, and to preserve it, "as much as lieth in you" (Romans 12:18), as much as you fairly and honorably can. This will have such an influence upon your conduct, as to make you not only cautious of giving offense, and slow in taking it, but earnestly desirous to regain peace as soon as may be, when it is in any measure broken, that the wound may be healed while it is green, and before it begins to rankle and fester. And more especially, this disposition will engage you "to keep the unity of the Spirit in the bond of peace" (Ephesians 4:3).

Philip Doddridge

36.6

Good deeds out of
sheer good will

Trust in the LORD and do good;
dwell in the land and enjoy safe pasture.
(PSALM 37:3)

The saintly children of God do their good deeds out of sheer good will, seeking no reward but alone God's honor and will, and are ready and eager to do good, and would be even if there were neither heaven nor hell. And this is proved fully by the words of Christ, when he says, "Come ye blessed of my Father, inherit the kingdom prepared for you from the foundation of the world." Now, could they merit, as reward of their deeds, that Kingdom, which is prepared for them before they are created? The Kingdom is not being prepared, for it is prepared already, but the children are being prepared for the Kingdom. . . . The Kingdom wins the children and not the children the Kingdom.

Martin Luther

THE WAY OF OBEDIENCE

Oh, that their hearts would be inclined to fear me and keep all my commands always, so that it might go well with them and their children forever!

(DEUTERONOMY 5:29)

One golden rule for spiritual discernment: Obedience

Now that you know these things,
you will be blessed if you do them.
(JOHN 13:17)

In spiritual matters, logical processes do not count. Curiosity does not count, nor argument, nor reasoning: These are of no avail for spiritual discernment. There is only one golden rule for spiritual discernment and that is obedience. We learn more by five minutes' obedience than by ten years' study. Logic and reasons are methods of expounding reality, but we do not get at reality by our intellect. Reality is only gotten at by our conscience. When we deal with the records of Christ, we are dealing with fundamental realities. And there is nothing logical about faith; it is of the nature of life.

Oswald Chambers

37.1

We are blessed indeed
if we obey

*Blessed are they who maintain justice,
who constantly do what is right.*
(PSALM 106:3)

My friends, if we keep God's commandments in a true loving comradeship together, so that our sins may be forgiven for that love's sake, we are blessed indeed. It is written, "Blessed are they whose iniquities are forgiven, and over whose sins a veil is drawn; blessed is the man of whose sins the Lord takes no account, and on whose lips there is no deceit." And this blessing were theirs who were chosen by God through Jesus Christ our Lord. To him be glory for ever and ever, amen.

Clement of Rome

37.2

A virtuous life makes us dear to God

Do what is right and good in the LORD's sight, so that it may go well with you and you may go in and take over the good land that the LORD promised on oath to your forefathers.
(DEUTERONOMY 6:18)

Surely high words do not make a man holy and just; but a virtuous life maketh him dear to God. I had rather feel compunction, than understand the definition thereof. If thou didst know the whole Bible by heart, and the sayings of all the philosophers, what would all that profit thee without the love of God and without grace? Vanity of vanities, and all is vanity, except to love God, and to serve him only. This is the highest wisdom, by contempt of the world to tend toward the kingdom of heaven.

Thomas à Kempis

37.3

Doing God's will: Our well-being

I gave them this command: Obey me,
and I will be your God and you will be my
people. Walk in all the ways I command you,
that it may go well with you.
(JEREMIAH 7:23)

It is in God's will that all true spirituality lies. It is in this that we make our spiritual progress. The more perfectly that we practice this, the more we shall receive from our Lord, and the further shall we advance in his way. But do not think that we have to use strange jargon or dabble in things of which we have knowledge or understanding. For our entire well-being is to be found in what I have just described, namely, doing God's will.

Teresa of Avila

37.4

Total loyalty

Not everyone who says to me, "Lord, Lord," will enter the kingdom of heaven, but only he who does the will of my Father who is in heaven.
(MATTHEW 7:21)

God has little patience with those weak souls who say to themselves, "I shall go this far and no farther." Is it up to the creature to make the law for his Creator? What would a king say of a subject, or a master of his servant, who only served him in his own way, who feared to care too much for his interests, and who was embarrassed in public because of belonging to him? Still more what will the King of Kings say if we act like these cowardly servants?

Fénelon

37.5

Peace comes from complete resignation to God

Submit yourselves, then, to God. Resist the devil, and he will flee from you.
(JAMES 4:7)

There will never be any peace for those who resist God. If there is any joy in the world, it is saved for the pure conscience. The whole earth is a place of tribulation and agony for a bad conscience. But the peace which comes from God is different from that which comes from the world. It calms our passions. It preserves the purity of our conscience. It is inseparable from justice. It unites with God. It strengthens us against temptation. . . . Temptation, if it does not overcome us, always carries its fruits with it. The soul's peace consists in an entire resignation to the will of God.

Fénelon

37.6

Truthfulness: the fullness
of discipleship

*Therefore each of you must put off falsehood
and speak truthfully to his neighbor, for we
are all members of one body.*
(EPHESIANS 4:25)

The commandment of absolute truthfulness is really
only another name for the fullness of discipleship.
Absolute truthfulness is possible only where sin has
been uncovered, that is to say, where it has been
forgiven by Jesus. Only those who are in a state of
truthfulness through the confession of their sin to
Jesus are not ashamed to tell the truth wherever it
must be told. . . . But sinful men do not like this sort
of truthfulness, and they resist it with all their might.
That is why they persecute it and crucify it. It is only
because we follow Jesus that we can be genuinely
truthful, for then he reveals to us our sin upon the
cross. The cross is God's truth about us, and therefore it is the only power which can make us truthful.

Dietrich Bonhoeffer

37.7

FIND HIS WILL AND DO IT

The world and its desires pass away,
but the man who does the will of God
lives forever.

(1 JOHN 2:17)

We come to God in complete abandonment

Obey them not only to win their favor when their eye is on you, but like slaves of Christ, doing the will of God from your heart.
(EPHESIANS 6:6)

Devotion and piety are apt to be the greatest opponents of Jesus Christ, because we devote ourselves to devotion instead of to him. To surrender to God is not to surrender to the fact that we have surrendered. This is not "coming" at all. To come means that we come to God in complete abandonment and give ourselves right over to him and leave ourselves in his hands. The Lord Jesus Christ is the one person to whom we ought to yield, and we must be perfectly certain that it is to himself that we are yielding. Do not be sorry if other appeals find you stiffnecked and unyielding; but be sorry if, when he says, "Come to me," you do not come. The attitude of coming is that the will resolutely lets go of everything and deliberately commits all to him.

Oswald Chambers

Independence a hindrance
to spirituality

Epaphras . . . is always wrestling in prayer
for you, that you may stand firm in all the
will of God, mature and fully assured.
(COLOSSIANS 4:12)

The characteristics of the natural man, apart from
sin, are independence and individuality. Individuality is the strong and emphatic and somewhat ugly
husk that guards the personal life. Individuality is a
right characteristic in a child, but in a man or woman
it is not only objectionable but dangerous, because
it means independence of God as well as of other
people, and independence of God is of the very
nature of sin. The only way we can get rid of the
pride of individuality and become one with Jesus
Christ is by being born from above.

Oswald Chambers

38.2

Leave the past to his mercy

Brothers, I do not consider myself yet to have taken hold of it. But one thing I do: Forgetting what is behind and straining toward what is ahead. . . .

(PHILIPPIANS 3:13)

As to those things which it still remains to say or do, we will think of those in their proper time, and God will provide for all; sufficient unto the day is the evil thereof; will not tomorrow and the next bring with them their peculiar graces? Let us then think only of the present and follow the order of God; let us leave the past to his mercy, the future to Providence, striving peaceably all the time and without anxiety, first of all for salvation; and for the rest, let us leave its success entirely to God, casting on his parental bosom all our vain anxieties.

J. P. de Caussade

Foolish emotions make conflicts

*Every prudent man acts out of knowledge,
but a fool exposes his folly.*
(PROVERBS 13:16)

We have only to follow God obediently, and to yield
entirely to God our mood, our own will, our sensi-
tiveness, our anxiety, our self-concern, as well as the
over-enthusiasm, the haste, the foolish joy, and
other emotions which make conflicts for us according to whether the things which we have to do are
agreeable or inconvenient.

Fénelon

Give up the toys

He chose to be mistreated along with the people of God rather than to enjoy the pleasures of sin for a short time.
(HEBREWS 11:25)

Father, I want to know thee, but my coward heart fears to give up its toys. I cannot part with them without inward bleeding, and I do not try to hide from thee the terror of the parting. I come trembling, but I do come. Please root from my heart all those things which I have cherished so long and which have become a very part of my living self, so that thou mayest enter and dwell there without a rival. Then shalt thou make the place of thy feet glorious. Then shall my heart have no need of the sun to shine in it, for thyself wilt be the light of it, and there shall be no night there.

A. W. Tozer

Purified, polished, and
perfected in his timing

I will praise you with an upright heart
as I learn your righteous laws.
(PSALM 119:7)

Now let me say something about being introspec-
tive. Dying to your self-nature is a command from
God. It plays a vital part in your relationship with
him and with others. However, a constant, inward
gaze should never be a primary, principal exercise of
a Christian. Your main focus should always be on
God and the activities involved in getting to know
him. God himself will show you the areas of your life
which need attention. Those who are faithfully
abandoning all to God will indeed be purified, pol-
ished, and perfected in his timing.

Jeanne Guyon

May his will be done on earth

You need to persevere so that when you have done the will of God, you will receive what he has promised.
(HEBREWS 10:36)

The great anxieties about which my mind had been exercised during my seasons of agonizing prayer, seemed to be set aside; so that for a long time when I went to God to commune with him—as I did very, very frequently—I would fall on my knees and find it impossible to ask for anything with any earnestness except that his will might be done on earth as it was done in heaven. My prayers were swallowed up in that; and I often found myself smiling, as it were, in the face of God, and saying that I did not want anything. I was very sure that he would accomplish all his wise and good pleasure; and with that my soul was entirely satisfied.

Charles G. Finney

CONTENT WITH GOD'S PROVISION

Not that I was ever in need, for I have learned how to get along happily whether I have much or little. I know how to live on almost nothing or with everything. I have learned the secret of contentment in every situation, whether it be a full stomach or hunger, plenty or want; for I can do everything God asks me to with the help of Christ who gives me the strength and power.

(PHILIPPIANS 4:11-13, TLB)

He asks us to accept our cross

*Put to death, therefore, whatever belongs to
your earthly nature: sexual immorality,
impurity, lust, evil desires and greed,
which is idolatry.*
(COLOSSIANS 3:5)

It is one thing to recognize what God is doing with
us, but another thing to deliberately accept it as his
appointment. We can never accept the appointment
of Jesus Christ and bear away the sin of the world;
that was his work. But he does ask us to accept our
cross. What is my cross? The manifestation of the
fact that I have given up my right to myself to him
forever. Self-interest, self-sympathy, self-pity—anything and everything that does not arise from a
determination to accept my life entirely from him
will lead to a dissipation of my life.

Oswald Chambers

39.1

Heavy-laden, thou art
near to God

*Come to me, all you who are weary
and burdened, and I will give you rest.
Take my yoke upon you and learn from me, for
I am gentle and humble in heart,
and you will find rest for your souls.*
(MATTHEW 11:28-29)

Better it is to be heavy-laden and near one that is strong than relieved of one's load and near one that is weak. When thou art heavy-laden, thou art near to God, who is thy strength and is with them that are in trouble. When thou art relieved, thou art near but to thyself, who are thine own weakness. For the virtue and strength of the soul grows and is confirmed by trials and patience. He that desires to be alone without the support of a master and guide will be like the tree that is alone in the field and has no owner. However much fruit it bears, passers-by will pluck it all, and it will not mature. . . . The soul that is alone and without a master, and has virtue, is like the burning coal that is alone. It will grow colder rather than hotter.

St. John of the Cross

39.2

Perfect confidence
in his goodness

He who did not spare his own Son, but gave him up for us all—how will he not also, along with him, graciously give us all things?
(ROMANS 8:32)

I had had a great struggle about giving up my wife to the will of God. She was in very feeble health, and it was very evident that she could not live long. I told the Lord that I had such confidence in him that I felt perfectly willing to give myself, my wife and my family, and all, to be disposed of without any qualification according to his own views and will. Indeed, I recollect that I went so far as to say to the Lord with all my heart, that he might do anything with me or mine to which his blessed will could consent. That I had such perfect confidence in his goodness and love, as to believe that he could consent to do nothing to which I could object. I felt a kind of holy boldness in telling him to do with me just as seemed to him good. . . . So deep and perfect a resting in the will of God I had never before known.

Charles G. Finney

39.3

Rejoice in the joy of others

There should be no division in the body, but that its parts should have equal concern for each other. If one part suffers, every part suffers with it; if one part is honored, every part rejoices with it.

(1 CORINTHIANS 12:25-26)

A few years after [a] season of refreshing . . . my beloved wife died. This was to me a great affliction. . . . One day I was upon my knees communing with God. . . . All at once he seemed to say: "You loved your wife?" "Yes," I said. "Well, did you love her for her own sake, or for your sake? . . . If you loved her for her own sake, why do you sorrow that she is with me? . . . Did you love her," he seemed to say to me, "for my sake? If you loved her for my sake, surely you would not grieve that she is with me. . . . If you loved her for her own sake, would you not rejoice in her joy and be happy in her happiness?" I can never describe the feelings that came over me. . . . It produced an instantaneous change in the whole state of my mind.

Charles G. Finney

39.4

Take everything as from the hand of God

The Lord gave me everything I had,
and they were his to take away.
Blessed be the name of the Lord.
(JOB 1:21, TLB)

Was not Job mistaken? Should he not have said: "The Lord gave, and Satan hath taken away"? No, there was no mistake. He was enabled to discern the hand of God in all these calamities. Satan himself did not presume to ask God to be allowed *himself* to afflict. He says to God: "Put forth *thine* hand now, and touch his flesh and bone, and he will curse thee to thy face." . . . Oftentimes shall we be helped and blessed if we bear this in mind—that Satan is *servant* and not *master*, and that he, and wicked men incited by him, are only permitted to do that which God by his determined counsel and foreknowledge had before determined should be done. Come joy or come sorrow, we may always take it from the hand of God.

J. Hudson Taylor

Look to the Lord to keep you

Unless the LORD builds the house, its builders labor in vain. Unless the LORD watches over the city, the watchmen stand guard in vain. In vain you rise early and stay up late, toiling for food to eat—for he grants sleep to those he loves.
(PSALM 127:1-2)

What will it profit a man if he gains his cause, and silences his adversary, if at the same time he loses that humble tender frame of spirit in which the Lord delights, and to which the promise of his presence is made! Your aim, I doubt not, is good, but you have need to watch and pray, for you will find Satan at your right hand to resist you; he will try to debase your views, and though you set out in defense of the cause of God, if you are not continually looking to the Lord to keep you, it will become your own cause, and awaken in you those tempers which are inconsistent with true peace of mind, and will surely obstruct communion with God.

John Newton

39.6

Don't seek out suffering

When you fast, do not look somber as the hypocrites do, for they disfigure their faces to show men they are fasting. I tell you the truth, they have received their reward in full. But when you fast, put oil on your head and wash your face, so that it will not be obvious to men that you are fasting, but only to your Father, who is unseen; and your Father, who sees what is done in secret, will reward you.

(MATTHEW 6:16-18)

Nothing is more false and more indiscreet than always to want to choose what mortifies us in everything. By this rule a person would soon ruin his health, his business, his reputation, his relations with his relatives and friends, in fact every good work which Providence gives him.

Fénelon

GROWING UP IN GOD'S FAMILY

Now it is God who makes both us and you stand firm in Christ. He anointed us, set his seal of ownership on us, and put his Spirit in our hearts as a deposit, guaranteeing what is to come.

(2 CORINTHIANS 1:21-22)

Maturity depends on obedience

Perseverance must finish its work so that you may be mature and complete, not lacking anything.
(JAMES 1:4)

Just when maturity is reached spiritually we cannot say; all we know is, it depends entirely on obedience. After they were baptized with the Holy Spirit, the early disciples evidently reached the point of spiritual maturity, for we read that they were "rejoicing that they were counted worthy to suffer shame for his name." They could not be appealed to on any other line than the one marked out for them by Jesus; it could not be tyrannized or martyred out of them. The baptism of our Lord represents this point of amazing maturity; we are faced with a revelation we cannot understand, but we must accept.

Oswald Chambers

Understanding God's
will is maturity

All of us who are mature should take
such a view of things. And if on some point
you think differently, that too
God will make clear to you.
(PHILIPPIANS 3:15)

Spiritual maturity is not reached by the passing of years, but by obedience to the will of God. Some people mature into an understanding of God's will more quickly than others because they obey more readily; they more readily sacrifice the life of nature to the will of God; they more easily swing clear of little, determined opinions. It is these little determined opinions, convictions of our own that won't budge, that hinder growth in grace and make us bitter and dogmatic, intolerant, and utterly unChristlike.

Oswald Chambers

40.2

Spiritually we never grow old

Therefore we do not lose heart. Though outwardly we are wasting away, yet inwardly we are being renewed day by day.
(2 CORINTHIANS 4:16)

Spiritually we never grow old; through the passing of things we grow so many years young. The characteristic of the spiritual life is its unaging youth, exactly the opposite of the natural life. "I am . . . the First and the Last." The Ancient of Days represents the eternal childhood. God Almighty became the weakest thing in his own creation, a baby. . . . The mature saint is just like a little child, absolutely simple and joyful and lively. Go on living the life that God would have you live, and you will grow younger instead of older. There is a marvelous rejuvenescence when once you let God have his way.

Oswald Chambers

Willing and hearty obedience

Anyone who breaks one of the least of these commandments and teaches others to do the same will be called least in the kingdom of heaven, but whoever practices and teaches these commands will be called great in the kingdom of heaven.
(MATTHEW 5:19)

Many live under obedience, rather for necessity than for charity; such are discontented, and do easily repine. Neither can they attain to freedom of mind, unless they willingly and heartily put themselves under obedience for the love of God. . . . Who is so wise that he can fully know all things? Be not therefore too confident in thine own opinion; but be willing to hear the judgment of others. . . . I have often heard that it is safer to hear and take counsel than to give it. It may also fall out that each one's opinion may be good, but to refuse to yield to others when reason or a special cause requireth it, is a sign of pride and stiffness.

Thomas à Kempis

40.4

We belong to the one we obey

Your own body does not belong to you.
For God has bought you with a great price.
So use every part of your body to give
glory back to God, because he owns it.
(1 CORINTHIANS 6:19-20, TLB)

Happy the soul which, by a sincere self-renuncia-
tion, holds itself ceaselessly in the hands of its Creator, ready to do everything which he wishes; which
never stops saying to itself a hundred times a day,
"Lord, what wouldst thou that I should do? Teach
me to perform thy holy will, for thou art God. Thou
wilt show that thou art my God by teaching me, and
I will show that I am thy creature by obeying thee."

Fénelon

Willing to be controlled

You were bought at a price;
do not become slaves of men.
(1 CORINTHIANS 7:23)

God is not satisfied by the sound of our lips, nor the position of our bodies, nor external ceremonies. What he asks is a will which will no longer be divided between him and any creature, a will pliant in his hands, which neither desires anything nor refuses anything, which wants without reservation everything which he wants, and which never, under any pretext, wants anything which he does not want.

Fénelon

40.6

What shall we give our Re-creator more?

Don't you know that when you offer yourselves to someone to obey him as slaves, you are slaves to the one whom you obey—whether you are slaves to sin, which leads to death, or to obedience, which leads to righteousness?
(ROMANS 6:16)

God certainly is well within his rights in claiming to himself the works of his own hands, the gifts he himself has given! How should the thing made fail to love the maker, provided that it have from him the power to love at all. . . . If then I owe myself entirely to my Creator, what shall I give my Re-creator more? The means of our remaking too, think what they cost! It was far easier to make than to redeem; for God had but to speak the word and all things were created, I concluded. . . . By his first work he gave me to myself; and by the next he gave himself to me. And when he gave himself, he gave me back myself that I had lost. . . . I doubly owe him. But what shall I return for myself? A thousand of myself would be as nothing in respect of him.

Bernard of Clairvaux
40.7

LIVING OUT WHAT WE BELIEVE

Whatever you have learned or received or heard from me, or seen in me—put it into practice. And the God of peace will be with you.

(PHILIPPIANS 4:9)

Indulge no more inward doubts

When you ask him, be sure that you really expect him to tell you, for a doubtful mind will be as unsettled as a wave of the sea that is driven and tossed by the wind.

(JAMES 1:6, TLB)

The all-merciful and beneficent Father is compassionate to those that fear him; to approach him in sincerity of heart is to be repaid with his kind and gracious favors. So let us be done with vacillation, and indulge no more inward doubts of the reality of his great and glorious gifts. . . . Consider as true, you unwise ones, and how apt a figure of yourselves it is. Look at the vine; it first casts its foliage, and then a bud appears, and next a leaf, and later a flower, and after that a young unripe grape, and then finally the full cluster. See how short a time it takes for the fruit to mature. Truly, his purpose will accomplish itself just as swiftly and suddenly.

Clement of Rome

41.1

Wait in patience for him

Brothers, as an example of patience in the face of suffering, take the prophets who spoke in the name of the Lord. As you know, we consider blessed those who have persevered.

(JAMES 5:10)

How blessed, how marvelous are the gifts of God, my friends! Some of them, indeed, already lie within our comprehension—the life that knows no death, the shining splendor of righteousness, the truth that is frank and full, the faith that is perfect assurance, the holiness of chastity—but what of the thing prepared for those who wait? Who but the Creator and Father of eternity, the Most Holy Himself, knows the greatness of the beauty of these? Let us strain every nerve to be found among those who wait in patience for him, so that we too may earn a share of his promised gifts. And how is this done, my friends? Why, by fixing our minds trustfully on God; by finding out what is pleasing and acceptable to him; by doing whatever agrees with his perfect will; by following the paths of truth.

Clement of Rome

41.2

Forsake your sins to find mercy

You have set our iniquities before you,
our secret sins in the light of your presence.
(PSALM 90:8)

No man living in any known sin is ever comforted of God. The Holy Ghost never yet spake one word of all his abounding consolations to any man so long as he lived in any actual sin, or in any neglect of known duty. . . . As long as you are living in any guilt, as long as your conscience accuses you, [God] will by no means clear or comfort you. "He that forsaketh his sins shall find mercy"—but he only. You do not really care for God's mercy or his comfort either, so long as you live in any sin. And it is well that you do not; for you can have neither. Your peace will be like a river when you put away your sin; but not one word of true peace, not one drop of true comfort, can you have till then.

Alexander Whyte

41.3

Rapid and happy progress through submission

Commit everything you do to the Lord.
Trust him to help you do it and he will.
(PSALM 37:5, TLB)

If souls had courage enough to resign themselves to the work of purification, without having any weak and foolish pity on themselves, what a noble, rapid, and happy progress would they make! But few are willing to lose the earth. If they advance some steps, as soon as the sea is ruffled they are dejected; they cast anchor, and often desist from the prosecution of the voyage. Such disorders doth selfish interest and self-love occasion. It is of consequence not to look too much at one's own state, not to lose courage, not to afford any nourishment to self-love, which is so deep-rooted, that its empire is not easily demolished.

Jeanne Guyon

41.4

Dependence on the Father

A father to the fatherless, a defender of widows, is God in his holy dwelling.
(PSALM 68:5)

Child of God, it is not only for the only begotten Son that a life plan has been arranged, but for each one of his children. Just in proportion as we live in more or less entire dependence on the Father will this life plan be more or less perfectly worked out in our lives. The nearer the believer comes to this entire dependence of the Son, "doing nothing but what he sees the Father do," and then to his implicit obedience, "whatsoever he doeth, doing these in like manner," so much more will the promise be fulfilled in us: "The Father showeth him all things that he himself doeth, and will show him greater works than these" [John 5:19-20].

Andrew Murray

Hope and quiet waiting

We depend upon the Lord alone to save us.
Only he can help us; he protects us like a
shield. No wonder we are happy in the Lord!
For we are trusting him. We trust his holy
name. Yes, Lord, let your constant love
surround us, for our hopes are in you alone.
(PSALM 33:20-22, TLB)

We associate hope with impulse; quiet waiting is
surely the want of impulse! Hope is a state of flight;
waiting implies repose. Hope is the soul on the
wing; waiting is the soul in the nest. Is not that
strange union of feelings to put into one breast! No;
it is a sublimely happy marriage. . . . There is no test
of hope like quiet waiting. . . . To measure the
strength of a man's hope, you must measure the
quietness of his waiting. Our hope is never so weak
as when we are excited. Two men . . . were equally
bent on the same cause. . . . The one was fiery,
impetuous, vehement, . . . the other was calm, cool,
quiet. . . . He was calm because he had seen the star
in the east, and he knew it was traveling westward.

George Matheson

41.6

Look to him to work
fruitfulness in us

*I myself will gather the remnant of my flock
out of all the countries where I have driven
them and will bring them back to their
pasture, where they will be fruitful
and increase in number.*

(JEREMIAH 23:3)

The word [in John 15:2] "more fruit" is most encouraging. Let us listen to it. It is just to the branch that is bearing fruit that the message comes: more fruit. God does not demand this as Pharaoh the taskmaster or as Moses the lawgiver, without providing the means. He comes as a Father, who gives what he asks, and works what he commands. He comes to us as the living branches of the living Vine, and offers to work the more fruit in us, if we but yield ourselves into his hands. Shall we not admit the claim, accept the offer, and look to him to work it in us? . . . God has set his heart on more fruit; Christ waits to work in us; let us joyfully look up to our divine Husbandman and our heavenly Vine, to ensure our bearing more fruit.

Andrew Murray

41.7

LOOKING HEAVENWARD

When the perishable has been clothed with the imperishable, and the mortal with immortality, then the saying that is written will come true: "Death has been swallowed up in victory." "Where, O death, is your victory? Where, O death, is your sting?" The sting of death is sin, and the power of sin is the law. But thanks be to God! He gives us the victory through our Lord Jesus Christ.

(1 CORINTHIANS 15:54-57)

Come together for spiritual improvement.

In Christ we who are many form one body,
and each member belongs to all the others.
We have different gifts, according to the grace
given us. If a man's gift is prophesying,
let him use it in proportion to his faith.
If it is serving, let him serve;
if it is teaching, let him teach.
(ROMANS 12:5-7)

Be watchful over your life; never let your lamps go out or your loins be ungirt, but keep yourselves always in readiness, for you can never be sure of the hour when our Lord may be coming. Come often together for spiritual improvement.

from The Didache

42.1

We rest at his sovereign disposal

As the eyes of slaves look to the hand of their
master, as the eyes of a maid look to the hand
of her mistress, so our eyes look to the LORD
our God, till he shows us his mercy.
(PSALM 123:2)

Some desire to live that they may see more of that glorious work of God for his church, which they believe he will accomplish. So Moses prayed that he might not die in the wilderness, but go over Jordan, and see the good land. . . . Paul knew not clearly whether it were not best for him to abide a while longer in the flesh on this account. . . . But no man can die cheerfully or comfortably who lives not in a constant resignation of the time and season of his death unto the will of God, as well as himself with respect unto death itself. Our times are in his hand, at his sovereign disposal, and his will in all things must be complied withal. Without this resolution, without this resignation, no man can enjoy the least solid peace in this world.

John Owen

42.2

We should be ready at all times

So you also must be ready, because the Son of Man will come at an hour when you do not expect him.
(MATTHEW 24:44)

St. Augustine says: "Nothing is so certain as death, and nothing is so uncertain as the hour of death." For wherever and however it may come, of the time and the hour knoweth no man. Therefore nothing can be more necessary than that we should be ready at all times, and that we should know that we are, and not only hope so. We have been placed in this life, not only to do the works, but also that we may know, so that our works may grow out of knowledge, as fruit grows out of the tree. Therefore our work in this life is to gain more knowledge, and so to come nearer to God.

Johann Tauler

42.3

Be prepared when he calls

But, dear brothers, you are not in the dark about these things, and you won't be surprised as by a thief when that day of the Lord comes. . . . Watch for his return and stay sober.
(1 THESSALONIANS 5:4, 6, TLB)

The approaches of death have especial trials which, unless we are prepared for them, will keep us under bondage with the fear of death itself. . . . Some who have been wholly freed from all fears of death . . . who have looked on it as amiable and desirable in itself, have yet had great exercise in their minds about these ways of its approach. . . . To get above all perplexities on the account of these things is part of our wisdom in dying daily. And we are to have always in readiness those graces and duties which are necessary thereunto. . . . So is it to live in the exercise of faith that if God calls us unto any of those things . . . he will give us such supplies of spiritual strength and patience as shall enable us to undergo them.

John Owen

42.4

We shall then see clearly

We can see and understand only a little about God now, as if we were peering at his reflection in a poor mirror; but someday we are going to see him in his completeness, face to face. Now all that I know is hazy and blurred, but then I will see everything clearly, just as clearly as God sees into my heart right now.

(1 CORINTHIANS 13:12, TLB)

We avoid the thought of death in order not to be saddened by it. It will only be sad for those who have not thought about it. It will come at last, this death, and will enlighten him who did not want to be enlightened during his life. We will have at death a very distinct light on all that we have done, and on all that we should have done. We shall see clearly the use which we should have made of the grace we have received, the talents, the wealth, the health, the time, and all the advantages or misfortunes of our life.

Fénelon

42.5

Death: The consummation of the work of grace

Now we know that if the earthly tent we live in is destroyed, we have a building from God, an eternal house in heaven, not built by human hands. Meanwhile we groan, longing to be clothed with our heavenly dwelling.

(2 CORINTHIANS 5:1-2)

We cannot too greatly deplore the blindness of those who do not want to think of death, and who turn away from an inevitable thing which we could be happy to think of often. Death only troubles carnal people. "Perfect love casts out fear." It is not by thinking ourselves right that we cease to fear. It is simply by loving, and abandoning ourselves to him who we love without returning to self. That is what makes death sweet and precious. When we are dead to ourselves, the death of the body is only the consummation of the work of grace.

Fénelon

Live and labor for other's welfare

Be devoted to one another in brotherly love.
Honor one another above yourselves.
(ROMANS 12:10)

If heaven is for the pure and holy, if that which makes men good is that which best qualifies for heaven, what better discipline in goodness can we conceive for a human spirit . . . than to live and labor for a brother's welfare? . . . Then, let death come when it may, and carry you where it will, you will not be unprepared for it. The rending of the veil which hides the secrets of the unseen world, the summons that calls you into regions unknown, need awaken in your breast no perturbation or dismay; for you cannot in God's universe go where love and truth and self-devotion are things of naught, or where a soul, filled with undying faith in the progress and identifying its own happiness with the final triumph of goodness, shall find itself forsaken.

John Caird

42.7

WORKING OUT CHRIST'S LIFE IN OURS

And I pray that as you share your faith with others it will grip their lives too, as they see the wealth of good things in you that come from Christ Jesus.

(PHILEMON 6, TLB)

Be yourselves your own good lawgivers

Therefore, it is necessary to submit to the authorities, not only because of possible punishment but also because of conscience.
(ROMANS 13:5)

The day is approaching when the world will share the fate of the Evil One. "The Lord is at hand, and his reward with him." So once again I must urge you: be yourselves your own good lawgivers, be yourself your own trusty counselors, and have no more to do with the piety of hypocrites. May the God and Lord of all the world grant you wisdom, understanding, and knowledge, together with true comprehension of his ordinances and the gift of perseverance. Take God for your teacher, and study to learn what the Lord requires of you; then do it, and you will find yourselves accepted at the Day of Judgment.

Barnabas

Salvation: Righteousness
made possible

Therefore, there is now no condemnation for those who are in Christ Jesus, because through Christ Jesus the law of the Spirit of life set me free from the law of sin and death.
(ROMANS 8:1-2)

Salvation is righteousness made possible. If you tell me that salvation is deliverance from hell, I tell you that you have an utterly inadequate understanding of what salvation is. If you tell me that salvation is forgiveness of sins, I shall affirm that you have a very partial understanding of what salvation is. Unless there be more in salvation than deliverance from the penalty and forgiveness of transgressions, then I solemnly say that salvation cannot satisfy my own heart and conscience. . . . Salvation, then, is making possible that righteousness. Salvation is the power to do right. However enfeebled the will may be, however polluted the nature, the gospel comes bringing to men the message of power enabling them to do right.

G. Campbell Morgan

43.2

Go higher

*He must not be a recent convert, or he may
become conceited and fall under the same
judgment as the devil. He must also have a
good reputation with outsiders, so that he will
not fall into disgrace and into the devil's trap.*
(1 TIMOTHY 3:6-7)

An elevated mood can only come out of an elevated
habit of personal character. If in the externals of your
life you live up to the highest you know, God will
continually say, "Friend, go up higher." The golden
rule in temptation is—Go higher. When you get
higher up, you face other temptations and characteristics. Satan used the strategy of elevation in
temptation, and God does the same, but the effect
is different. When the devil puts you in an elevated
place, he makes you screw your idea of holiness
beyond what flesh and blood could ever bear. . . .
But when God elevates you by his grace into the
heavenly places, instead of finding a pinnacle to cling
to, you find a great tableland where it is easy to
move.

Oswald Chambers

43.3

He can deliver us from besetting sin

It is for freedom that Christ has set us free.
Stand firm, then, and do not let yourselves be
burdened again by a yoke of slavery.
(GALATIANS 5:1)

If there is some sin that is getting the mastery over you, you certainly cannot be useful. You certainly cannot bring forth fruit to the honor and glory of God until you get self-control. "He that ruleth his spirit is better than he that taketh a city." . . . There isn't any evil within or without but what he will deliver us from it if we will let him. That is what he wants to do. As God said to Moses, "I have come down to deliver." If he could deliver three million slaves from the hands of the mightiest monarch on earth, don't you think he can deliver us from every besetting sin, and give us complete victory over ourselves, over our temper, over our dispositions, over our irritableness and peevishness and snappishness? If we want it and desire it above everything else, we can get victory.

Dwight L. Moody

43.4

Jesus Christ, my righteousness

For if, by the trespass of the one man, death
reigned through that one man, how much more
will those who receive God's abundant
provision of grace and of the
gift of righteousness reign in life
through the one man, Jesus Christ.
(ROMANS 5:17)

But one day, as I was passing in the field, and that
too with some dashes on my conscience, fearing lest
yet all was not right, suddenly this sentence fell upon
my soul, *Thy righteousness is in heaven;* and me-
thought withal, I saw, with the eyes of my soul, Jesus
Christ at God's right hand. . . . So when I came
home, I looked to see if I could find that sentence,
Thy righteousness is in heaven, but could not find such
a saying; wherefore my heart began to sink again;
only that was brought to my remembrance, "He is
made unto us of God wisdom, and righteousness,
and sanctification and redemption"; by this word I
saw the other sentence true. For by this Scripture I
saw that the Man Christ Jesus . . . is our righteousness and sanctification before God.

John Bunyan

43.5

We walk by faith

We live by faith, not by sight.
(2 CORINTHIANS 5:7)

A gilt-edged saint is no good, he is abnormal, unfit for daily life, and altogether unlike God. We are here as men and women, not as half-fledged angels, to do the work of the world, and to do it with an infinitely greater power to stand the turmoil because we have been born from above. If we try to reintroduce the rare moments of inspiration, it is a sign that it is not God we want. We are making a fetish of the moments when God did come and speak, and insisting he must do it again; whereas what God wants us to do is to walk by faith. . . . Never live for the rare moments, they are surprises. God will give us touches of inspiration when he sees we are not in danger of being led away by them. We must never make our moments of inspiration our standard; our standard is our duty.

Oswald Chambers

43.6

God's work in us

And now may the God of peace, who brought
again from the dead our Lord Jesus, equip you
with all you need for doing his will. May he who
became the great Shepherd of the sheep by an
everlasting agreement between God and you,
signed with his blood, produce in you through
the power of Christ all that is pleasing to him.
To him be glory forever and ever. Amen.
(HEBREWS 13:20-21, TLB)

In carrying out his great work in the world, God
works through human agents. . . . In order that they
may be effective agents, they must be "vessels unto
honor, sanctified, and meet for the master's use, and
prepared unto every good work." His work makes
progress in the hands of praying men. Peter tells us
that husbands who might not be reached by the
Word of God, might be won by the conduct of their
wives. It is those who are "blameless and harmless,
the sons of God," who can hold forth the word of
life "in the midst of a crooked and perverse nation."
The world judges religion not by what the Bible says,
but by how Christians live.

E. M. Bounds

43.7

DISCIPLINED FOR GROWTH

Come, let us return to the LORD.
He has torn us to pieces
but he will heal us; he has injured us
but he will bind up our wounds.
After two days he will revive us;
on the third day he will restore us,
that we may live in his presence.

(HOSEA 6:1-2)

Evil exists to bring about
a greater good

*Know then in your heart that as a man
disciplines his son, so the Lord your God
disciplines you. . . . He brought you water out
of hard rock. He gave you manna to eat in the
desert, something your fathers had never known,
to humble and to test you so that
in the end it might go well with you.*

(DEUTERONOMY 8:5, 15-16)

It is useless to say, "God's in his heaven; all's right
with the world," when many things are obviously all
wrong in the world. . . . This world exists for the
realization in time of God's eternal purposes. . . .
The manifold evils in the world are allowed to exist
because only through them can the greater good be
brought into activity. This greater good is not an
external achievement, but the love and heroism and
self-sacrifice which the great conflict calls into play.
We must return to the dauntless spirit of the early
Christians. . . . And let us remember, when we are
inclined to be disheartened, that the private soldier
is a poor judge of the fortunes of a great battle.

W. R. Inge

44.1

Jesus Christ our Lord,
Advocate, Mediator

God is on one side and all the people on the other side, and Christ Jesus, himself man, is between them to bring them together, by giving his life for all mankind.
(1 TIMOTHY 2:5, TLB)

Since no man is worthy to present himself to God and come into his sight, the heavenly Father himself, to free us at once from shame and fear, which might well have thrown our hearts into despair, has given us his Son, Jesus Christ our Lord, to be our advocate and mediator with him, by whose guidance we may confidently come to him, and with such an intercessor, trusting nothing we ask in his name will be denied us, as nothing can be denied to him by the Father. . . . For just as the promise commends Christ the Mediator to us, so, unless the hope of obtaining our requests depends upon him, it cuts itself off from the benefit of prayer.

John Calvin

44.2

A steep ascent requires labor and resolution

Do you not know that in a race all the runners run, but only one gets the prize? Run in such a way as to get the prize. . . . Therefore I do not run like a man running aimlessly; I do not fight like a man beating the air.
(1 CORINTHIANS 9:24, 26)

Heaven is above thee, and dost thou think to travel this steep ascent without labor and resolution? Canst thou get that earthly heart to heaven and bring that backward mind to God, while thou liest still and takest thine ease? If lying down at the foot of a hill and looking toward the top and wishing we were there would serve the turn, then we should have daily travelers for heaven. But the "kingdom of heaven suffereth violence, and violent men take it by force." There must be violence used to get these firstfruits, as well as to get the full possession. Dost thou not feel it is, though I should not tell thee? Will thy heart get upwards, except thou drive it?

Richard Baxter

44.3

God brings good out of evil

*I used to wander off until you punished me;
now I closely follow all you say. You are good
and do only good; make me follow your lead.*
(PSALM 119:67-68, TLB)

I believe that God can and will bring good out of
evil, even out of the greatest evil. For that purpose
he needs men who make the best use of everything.
I believe that God will give us all the strength we
need to help us resist in all time of distress. But he
never gives it in advance, lest we should rely on
ourselves and not on him alone. A faith such as this
should allay all our fears for the future. I believe that
even our mistakes and shortcomings are turned to
good account, and that it is no harder for God to
deal with them than with our supposedly good
deeds. I believe that God is no timeless fate, but that
he waits for and answers sincere prayers and responsible actions.

Dietrich Bonhoeffer

One deed of mercy worth more than many tears

"I tell you the truth," he said, "this poor widow has put in more than all the others. All these people gave their gifts out of their wealth; but she out of her poverty put in all she had to live on."

(LUKE 21:3-4)

Let us take warning from that fickle multitude who cried first Hosanna, then Crucify. A miracle startled them into a sudden adoration of their Savior—its effects on them soon died away. . . . Let us not be content with saying, "Lord, Lord," without "doing the things which he says." . . . One secret act of self-denial, one sacrifice of inclination of duty, is worth all the mere good thoughts, warm feelings, passionate prayers, in which idle people indulge themselves. It will give us more comfort on our deathbed to reflect on one deed of self-denying mercy, purity, or humility, than to recollect the shedding of many tears . . . and much spiritual exultation. . . . Good actions are the fruits of faith. . . . By them we shall be judged in the last day.

John Henry Newman

44.5

We must be better
than the rabble

So do not worry, saying, "What shall we eat?"
or "What shall we drink?" or "What shall we
wear?" For . . . your heavenly Father knows
that you need them. But seek first his kingdom
and his righteousness, and all these
things will be given to you as well.
(MATTHEW 6:31-33)

Unless we have the courage to fight for a revival of wholesome reserve between man and man, we shall perish in an anarchy of human values. The impudent contempt for such reserve is the mark of the rabble, just as inward uncertainty, haggling and cringing for the favor of insolent people, and lowering oneself to the level of the rabble are the way of becoming no better than the rabble oneself. When . . . the feeling for human quality and the power to exercise reserve cease to exist, chaos is at the door. When we tolerate impudence for the sake of material comforts, then we abandon our self-respect, the flood-gates are opened, chaos bursts the dam that we are to defend; and we are responsible for it all.

Dietrich Bonhoeffer

44.6

The law of gradual growth

*The path of the righteous is like the first
gleam of dawn, shining ever brighter
till the full light of day.*
(PROVERBS 4:18)

Man, in his spiritual nature too, is under the law of
gradual growth that reigns in all created life. It is
only in the path of development that he can reach
his divine destiny. And it is the Father, whose hands
are the times and seasons, who knows the moment
when the soul or the Church is ripened to that
fullness of faith in which it can really take and keep
the blessing. As a father who longs to have his only
child home from school, and yet waits patiently till
the time of training is completed, so it is with God
and his children; he is the long-suffering One, and
answers speedily.

Andrew Murray

Traveling with a Powerful God

I am the LORD, the God of all mankind. Is anything too hard for me?

(JEREMIAH 32:27)

God will not desert
his faithful ones

*So do not fear, for I am with you; do not be
dismayed, for I am your God. I will
strengthen you and help you; I will uphold you
with my righteous right hand.*
(ISAIAH 41:10)

Again, it is complained, many Christians have been
led into captivity. This would be lamentable, indeed,
if they had been led to a place where they could not
find their God. But Holy Scripture gives us instances
of great consolations bestowed even in such calamity. There were the three boys, Daniel, and other
Prophets who suffered captivity, but in no case was
God's comfort lacking. In like manner, the same
God who did not abandon the Prophet Jonah even
in the belly of a monster did not desert his faithful
ones in the power of a barbarous people, who were,
at least, human.

Augustine of Hippo

45.1

He rides upon the storms

Sing to God, O kingdoms of the earth,
sing praise to the LORD,
to him who rides the ancient skies above,
who thunders with mighty voice.
(PSALM 68:32-33)

God never thwarts adverse circumstances; that is not his method. I have often been struck with these words—"He rideth upon the wings of the wind." They are most suggestive. Our God does not *beat down* the storms that rise against him; he rides upon them; he works through them. You are often surprised that so many thorny paths are allowed to be open for the good—how that aspiring boy Joseph is put into a dungeon—how that beautiful child Moses is cast into the Nile. You would have expected Providence to have interrupted the opening of these pits destined for destruction. Well, he might have done so; he might have said to the storm, "Peace, be still!" But there was a more excellent way—to ride upon it.

George Matheson

45.2

Spiritual exercises
build confidence

Physical training is of some value,
but godliness has value for all things,
holding promise for both the present life
and the life to come.

(1 TIMOTHY 4:8)

All our spiritual exercises, of whatever nature they may be, are so many means of acquiring confidence in God. They all let us deeper down into him. They all unfold more and more of the nature of grace, and of the poverty of our own nature. . . . Our simple perseverance in anything good is a process of argumentation of our confidence. Outward temptations help us. They frighten us away from self-trust. They make us better acquainted with our possibilities of sin. They reveal to us in an alarming manner the vigor and the unweariness of the spiritual powers, which are arrayed against us. . . . Inward trials lead to the same result, only still more swiftly and more infallibly. God's arms are more closely folded round us in interior trials, than in the sensible sweetness of his consoling visitations. A much tried man is always a man of unbounded faith.

Frederick William Faber

45.3

The power of God's words

For the word of God is living and active.
Sharper than any double-edged sword,
it penetrates even to dividing soul and spirit,
joints and marrow; it judges the thoughts
and attitudes of the heart.
(HEBREWS 4:12)

It is a dreadful thing for a man to discover that much of his Christian work has been done in the power of his own natural life—his carnal nature. It is a dreadful thing for people who are naturally "capable," when God breaks up the things they have been relying upon—a natural gift of words, perhaps—but he must deal with that before he can clothe you with his own power. What a grand thing it would be if we all lost our power to "talk"! There is a "natural" flow of words that hinders the Spirit of God. Half a dozen words from the Book, and ten thousand words about it! Will you allow the Lord to take the knife of the Cross to this superfluity of words? He can never pour out through us the "rivers of living water" until that is done.

Jessie Penn-Lewis

45.4

The desire for his glory

In love he predestined us to be adopted as his
sons through Jesus Christ, in accordance with
his pleasure and will—to the praise of his
glorious grace, which he has freely
given us in the One he loves.
(EPHESIANS 1:4-6)

It is true that [God] wishes our happiness, but our
happiness is neither the true aid of his work, nor an
aim equal to that of his glory. It is indeed for his
glory that he wishes our happiness. Our happiness is
only a lesser aim, which he connects with the last and
essential aim, which is his glory. He himself is his
chief and only end in all things. To reach this main
aim of our creation, we must prefer God to ourselves, and only wish for our own salvation for the
sake of his glory. Otherwise we should reverse his
order. It is not our own interest in our blessedness
which should make us desire his glory. It is, on the
contrary, the desire for his glory which should make
us desire our blessedness, as one of the things which
he is pleased to make part of his glory.

Fénelon

45.5

We are supernatural people

You, dear children, are from God and have overcome them, because the one who is in you is greater than the one who is in the world.

(1 JOHN 4:4)

God's power is available power. We are supernatural people, born again by a supernatural birth, kept by a supernatural power, sustained on supernatural food, taught by a supernatural Teacher from a supernatural Book. We are led by a supernatural Captain in right paths to assured victories. The risen Savior, ere he ascended on high said, "All power is given unto Me. Go ye therefore." Again he said to his disciples: "Ye shall receive power when the Holy Spirit is come upon you." . . . The power given is not a gift from the Holy Spirit. He himself is the power. Today, he is as truly available and as mighty in power as he was on the day of Pentecost. . . . We have given too much attention to method, and to machinery, and to resources, and too little to the source of power.

J. Hudson Taylor

45.6

We produce work; the Spirit produces fruit

You did not choose me, but I chose you and appointed you to go and bear fruit—fruit that will last. Then the Father will give you whatever you ask in my name.
(JOHN 15:16)

Have you ever noticed the difference in the Christian life between work and fruit? A machine can do work; only life can bear fruit. A law can compel work; only love can spontaneously bring forth fruit. World implies effort and labor; the essential idea of fruit is that it is the silent natural produce of our inner life. The gardener may labor to give his apple tree the digging and manuring, the watering and the pruning it needs; he can do nothing to produce the apples; the tree bears its own fruit. So in the Christian life: "The fruit of the Spirit is love, peace, joy." The healthy life bears much fruit.

Andrew Murray

His Love Sets the Example

*I am giving a new commandment to
you now—love each other just as much
as I love you. Your strong love for each
other will prove to the world that you
are my disciples.*

(JOHN 13:34-35, TLB)

We love those whom he loves

For if anyone with a weak conscience sees you who have this knowledge eating in an idol's temple, won't he be emboldened to eat what has been sacrificed to idols? So this weak brother, for whom Christ died, is destroyed by your knowledge.
(1 CORINTHIANS 8:10-11)

Christ stood forth as the representative of men; . . . he identified himself with the cause and with the interests of all human beings . . . to lay down his life for them. Few of us sympathize originally and directly with this devotion; few of us can perceive in human nature itself any merit sufficient to evoke it. But it is not so hard to love and venerate him who felt it. So vast a passion of love, of devotion so comprehensive, has not elsewhere been in any degree approached, save by some of his imitators. . . . It matters no longer what quality men may exhibit; amiable or unamiable, as the brothers of Christ, as belonging to his sacred and consecrated kind, as the objects of his love in life and death, they must be dear to all to whom he is dear.

Sir John Seeley

46.1

Love to others: The door
out of the dungeon

*No one has ever seen God; but if we love one
another, God lives in us and
his love is made complete in us.*
(1 John 4:12)

The love of our neighbor is the only door out of the dungeon of self. . . . The man thinks his consciousness is himself; whereas his life consisteth in the inbreathing of God, and the consciousness of the universe of truth. To have himself, to know himself, to enjoy himself, he calls life; whereas, if he would forget himself, tenfold would be his life in God and his neighbors. The region of man's life is a spiritual region. God, his friends, his neighbors, his brothers all, is the wide world in which alone his spirit can find room. Himself is his dungeon. If he feels it not now, he will yet feel it one day—feel it as a living soul would feel being prisoned in a dead body. . . . His health is in the body of which the Son of Man is the head.

George Macdonald

46.2

The surest sign of
our love to God

If anyone says, "I love God," yet hates his brother, he is a liar. For anyone who does not love his brother, whom he has seen, cannot love God, whom he has not seen.
(1 JOHN 4:20)

There are only two duties that our Lord requires of us: the love of God, and the love of our neighbor. And, in my opinion, the surest sign for our discovering our love to God is discovering our love to our neighbor. Be assured that the further you advance in the love of your neighbor, the more you are advancing in the love of God. But alas, how many worms lie gnawing at the roots of our love to our neighbor! Self-love, self-esteem, fault-finding, envy, anger, impatience, and scorn. I assure you I write this with great grief, seeing myself to be so miserable a sinner against all my neighbors.

Teresa of Avila

Christ's example, our rule of life

Therefore, he who rejects this instruction does not reject man but God, who gives you his Holy Spirit. Now about brotherly love we do not need to write to you, for you yourselves have been taught by God to love each other.
(1 THESSALONIANS 4:8-9)

The believer who prays that his love may abound in knowledge, and really takes Christ's example as his rule of life, will be taught what a great and glorious work there is for him to do. The Church of God, and every child of God, as well as the world, have an unspeakable need for love, of the manifestation of Christ's love. The Christian who really takes the Lord's word, "Love one another, even as I have loved you," as a command that must be obeyed, carries about a power for blessing and life for all with whom he comes in contact. Love is the explanation of the whole wonderful life of Christ, and of the wonder of his death: Divine Love in God's children will still work its mighty wonders.

Andrew Murray

46.4

Wisdom: Love good
and hate evil

I, wisdom, dwell together with prudence; I possess knowledge and discretion. To fear the LORD is to hate evil; I hate pride and arrogance, evil behavior and perverse speech.
(PROVERBS 8:12-13)

Love the sovereign good, hate all evil and you will be truly wise. When you love anyone, is it because you know the reasons of love and its definitions? No, certainly. You love because your heart is formed to love what it finds amiable. Surely you cannot but know that there is nought lovely in the universe but God. Know ye not that he has created you, that he has died for you? But if these reasons are not sufficient, which of you has not some necessity, some trouble, or some misfortune? Which of you does not know how to tell his malady, and beg relief? Come, then, to this Fountain of all good, without complaining to weak and impotent creatures, who cannot help you; come to pray; lay before God your troubles, beg his grace—and above all, that you may love him.

Jeanne Guyon

46.5

To see and speak as Providence directs

Self-control means controlling the tongue!
A quick retort can ruin everything.
(PROVERBS 13:3, TLB)

Often the idea which a man falsely conceives of the greatness of his advancement in divine experience makes him want to be seen and known of men, and to wish to see the very same perfection in others. He conceives too low ideas of others, and too high of his own state. Then it becomes a pain to him to converse with people too human; whereas, a soul truly mortified and resigned would rather converse with the worst, by the order of Providence, than with the best, of its own choice; wanting only to see or to speak to any as Providence directs, knowing well that all beside, far from helping, only hurt it, or at least prove very unfruitful of it.

Jeanne Guyon

46.6

Meekness from humility,
anger from pride

*Pride leads to arguments; be humble,
take advice and become wise.*
(PROVERBS 13:10, TLB)

Jesus Christ said that we must be meek and humble
in heart. Meekness is the daughter of humility, as
anger is the daughter of pride. Only Jesus Christ can
give that true humility of heart that comes from him.
It is born of the unction of grace. It does not consist,
as one imagines, in performing exterior acts of humility, although that is good, but in keeping one's
place. He who has a high opinion of himself is not
truly humble. He who wants something for himself
is no more so. . . . But he, who does not seek his
own interest, but the interest of God alone in time
and eternity, is humble. The more we love purely,
the more perfect is our humility.

Fénelon

THE DUTIES OF LOVE

The goal of this command is love, which comes from a pure heart and a good conscience and a sincere faith.

(1 TIMOTHY 1:5)

The Son infinitely
worthy of love

The Father loves the Son and
has placed everything in his hands.
(JOHN 3:35)

As we think of the love of the Father to the Son, we see in the Son everything so infinitely worthy of that love. When we think of Christ's love to us, there is nothing but sin and unworthiness to meet the eye. And the question comes, How can that love within the bosom of the Divine life and its perfections be compared to the love that rests on sinners? Can it indeed be the same love? Blessed be God, we know it is so. The nature of love is always one, however different the objects. Christ knows of no law of love but that with which his Father loved him. Our wretchedness only serves to call out more distinctly the beauty of love.

Andrew Murray

47.1

Bury evil affections
in good works

If you love those who love you,
what reward will you get? Are not even
the tax collectors doing that?
(MATTHEW 5:46)

Never hold aloof from others because their conversation is not altogether to your taste. Love them, and they will love you, and then they will converse with you, and will become like you, and better than you. Let not your soul coop itself up in a corner. Or, instead of attaining to greater sanctity in proud, disdainful, and impatient seclusion, the devil will keep you company there. As so he will do your sequestered soul much mischief. Bury evil affections in good works. Therefore, be accessible and affable to all, and love all. Love is an endless enchantment; it is a spell and a fascination.

Teresa of Avila

God's love bears his
infinite character

*My command is this: Love each other as I have
loved you. Greater love has no one than this,
that he lay down his life for his friends.*
(JOHN 15:12-13)

The love which [God] has for us bears his infinite
character. He does not love as we do, with a limited
and narrow love. When he loves, the dimensions of
his love are infinite. He descends from heaven to
earth to seek the creature of clay, which he loves. He
becomes man and clay with him. He gives him his
flesh to eat. It is by such wonders of love that the
infinite surpasses all the affection of which men are
capable. He loves as a God, and this love is entirely
incomprehensible. It is the height of folly to wish to
measure infinite love by limited knowledge. Far
from losing any of his greatness by this excess of
love, he engraves it with the character of his greatness, marking it with the exuberance and ecstasy of
any infinite love. O how great and amiable he is in
his mysteries!

Fénelon

47.3

Faith the beginning,
love the end

And now these three remain: faith, hope and love. But the greatest of these is love.
(1 CORINTHIANS 13:13)

Given a thorough-going faith and love for Jesus Christ, there is nothing in all this that will not be obvious to you; for life begins and ends with these two qualities. Faith is the beginning and love is the end; and the union of the two together is God. All that makes for a soul's perfection follows in their train, for nobody who professes faith will commit sin, and nobody who possesses love can feel hatred. As the tree is known by its fruits, so they who claim to belong to Christ are known by their actions; for this work of ours does not consist in just making professions, but in a faith that is both practical and lasting.

Ignatius of Antioch

47.4

Serve God gladly within our limitations

Stone is heavy and sand a burden, but provocation by a fool is heavier than both. Anger is cruel and fury overwhelming, but who can stand before jealousy? Better is open rebuke than hidden love.

(PROVERBS 27:3-5)

Sometimes a man will be envious of that in others which will never be his, and can never be his. One who, in the providence of God, is only averagely endowed in respect of physique or intellect, or whom misfortune has gravely handicapped, may never settle down to accept his limitations and serve God gladly within them, but may go about all his life in a state of resentful bitterness and envy. All the while it is open to him, the second-rater, to be first-rate in magnanimity, to honor and love those who eclipse him in every respect, and who will eclipse him to the end of the chapter.

Archibald C. Craig

47.5

Love animates our action

Now that you have purified yourselves by obeying the truth so that you have sincere love for your brothers, love one another deeply, from the heart. For you have been born again, not of perishable seed, but of imperishable, through the living and enduring word of God.
(1 PETER 1:22-23)

Great works do not always lie in our way, but every moment we may do little ones excellently, that is, with great love. I beg you to mark the saint who gives a cup of water for God's sake to a poor thirsty traveler; he seems to do a small thing; but the intention, the sweetness, the love with which he animates his action, is so excellent that it turns this simple water into the water of life. . . . Truly in small and insignificant exercises of devotion charity is practices not only more frequently, but also as a rule more humbly too, and consequently more holily and usefully. . . . All this is more profitable to our souls that we can conceive, if heavenly love only has the management of them.

St. Francis de Sales

47.6

Everything from his hand

You have granted him the desire of his heart
and have not withheld the request of his lips.
You welcomed him with rich blessings
and placed a crown of pure gold on his head.
He asked you for life, and you gave it to
him—length of days, for ever and ever.
(PSALM 21:2-4)

By this pure dependence on his Spirit, everything is given us admirably. Our very weaknesses, in his hand, prove a source of humiliation. If the soul were faithful to leave itself in the hand of God, sustaining all his operations whether gratifying or mortifying, suffering itself to be conducted, from moment to moment by his hand, and annihilated by the strokes of his providence, without complaining, or desiring anything but what it has; it would soon arrive at the experience of the eternal truth, though it might not at once know the ways and methods by which God conducted it there.

Jeanne Guyon

GOD SEES US, FORGIVES US, AND ENCOURAGES US

Remember these things, O Jacob, for you are my servant, O Israel. I have made you, you are my servant; O Israel, I will not forget you. I have swept away your offenses like a cloud, your sins like the morning mist. Return to me, for I have redeemed you.

(ISAIAH 44:21-22)

48.0

We must see ourselves
as God sees us

*My frame was not hidden from you when I was
made in the secret place. When I was woven
together in the depths of the earth, your eyes
saw my unformed body. All the days ordained
for me were written in your book
before one of them came to be.*
(PSALM 139:15-16)

The sudden realization of his personal depravity
came like a stroke from heaven upon the trembling
heart of Isaiah at the moment when he had his
revolutionary vision of the holiness of God. His
pain-filled cry, "Woe is me! for I am undone." . . .
Until we have seen ourselves as God sees us, we are
not likely to be much disturbed over conditions
around us as long as they do not get so far out of
hand as to threaten our comfortable way of life. We
have learned to live with unholiness and have come
to look upon it as the natural and expected thing.

A. W. Tozer

48.1

God prizes humble hearts

The sacrifices of God are a broken spirit;
a broken and contrite heart,
O God, you will not despise.
(PSALM 51:17)

God puts a great price on humility of heart. It is good to be clothed with humility as with a garment. It is written, "God resisteth the proud, but giveth grace to the humble." That which brings the praying soul near to God is humility of heart. That which gives wings to prayer is lowliness of mind. That which gives ready access to the throne of grace is self-depreciation. Pride, self-esteem, and self-praise effectually shut the door of prayer. He who would come to God must approach him with self hid from his own eyes. He must not be puffed up with self-conceit, nor be possessed with an over-estimate of his virtues and good works.

E. M. Bounds

You are what you are before God

His eyes are on the ways of men; he sees their every step. There is no dark place, no deep shadow, where evildoers can hide. God has no need to examine men further, that they should come before him for judgment.

(JOB 34:21-23)

Blessed are you, servant of God, if you do not consider yourself any better when you are honored and extolled by others than when you are considered low and simple and despised; for what you are before God, that is what you are, and no more.

Francis of Assisi

48.3

Modest at all points

For by the grace given me I say to every one of you: Do not think of yourself more highly than you ought, but rather think of yourself with sober judgment, in accordance with the measure of faith God has given you.
(ROMANS 12:3)

Do not exaggerate your own importance, but be modest at all points, and never claim credit for yourself. Cherish no ill-natured designs upon your neighbor. Forbid yourself any appearance of presumption. . . . If you have to rebuke anyone for a fault, do it without fear or favor. Keep calm and mild; reverence the words you have heard, and bear no resentment toward a brother.

Barnabas

48.4

We owe all to pardoning grace

*By the grace of God I am what I am,
and his grace to me was not without effect.
No, I worked harder than all of them—yet not
I, but the grace of God that was with me.*
(1 CORINTHIANS 15:10)

The redeemed saint can never forget, either here or in eternity, that he is a forgiven sinner. Nothing works more mightily to inflame his love, to awaken his joy, or to strengthen his courage, than the experience, continually renewed by the Holy Spirit as a living reality, of God's forgiving love. Every day, yes, every thought of God reminds him: I owe all to pardoning grace. This forgiving love is one of the greatest marvels in the manifestation of the divine nature. In it God finds his glory and blessedness. And it is in this glory and blessedness God wants his redeemed people to share, when he calls upon them, as soon and as much as they have received forgiveness, also to bestow it upon others.

Andrew Murray

48.5

With what speed
didst thou come

I, even I, am he who blots out your transgressions, for my own sake, and remembers your sins no more.
(ISAIAH 43:25)

I fell then into the greatest of all misfortunes. I wandered yet farther and farther from thee, O my God, and thou didst gradually retire from a heart which had quitted thee. Yet such is thy goodness, that it seemed as if thou hadst left me with regret; and when this heart was desirous to return again unto thee, with what speed didst thou come to meet it. This proof of thy love and mercy shall be to me an everlasting testimony of thy goodness and of my own ingratitude.

Jeanne Guyon

48.6

Forgiveness, a reason for perpetual praise

Blessed is he whose transgressions are forgiven, whose sins are covered. Blessed is the man whose sin the LORD does not count against him and in whose spirit is no deceit.
(PSALM 32:1-2)

The feast which Levi gave to our Lord on his conversion is such a cheerful type to me of the Christian life. It is a festival of joy and gratitude for a conversion. We are sinners forgiven; there is a reason for perpetual praise. A feast represents a forgiven sinner's whole course; he is welcomed home, and he has brought more joy to heaven than there was before. His sorrow for sin is not a mortified, humiliated, angry disgust with himself. It is a humble, hopeful sorrow, always "turning into joy.". . . If we are sinners forgiven, we ought to behave as forgiven, welcomed home, crowned with wonderful love in Christ, and so cheer and encourage all about us, who often go heavily because we reflect our gloom upon them instead of our grateful love, hope, confidence.

Father Congreve

48.7

LOVING AND FORGIVING AS HE FORGAVE

And do not grieve the Holy Spirit of God, with whom you were sealed for the day of redemption. Get rid of all bitterness, rage and anger, brawling and slander, along with every form of malice. Be kind and compassionate to one another, forgiving each other, just as in Christ God forgave you.

(EPHESIANS 4:30-32)

Purged of all earthly preferences

To him who loves us and has freed us from our sins by his blood, and has made us to be a kingdom and priests to serve his God and Father—to him be glory and power for ever and ever! Amen.
(REVELATION 1:5-6)

See then, dear friends, what a great and wondrous thing love is. Its perfection is beyond all words. Who is fit to be called its possessor, but those whom God deems worthy? Let us beg and implore of his mercy that we may be purged of all earthly preferences for this man or that, and be found faultless in love. Though every generation from Adam to the present day has passed from the earth, yet such of them as by God's grace were perfected in love have their place now in the courts of the godly, and at the visitation of Christ's kingdom they will be openly revealed.

Clement of Rome

Living in the fear and love of God

As the Father has loved me, so have I loved you. Now remain in my love. If you obey my commands, you will remain in my love, just as I have obeyed my Father's commands and remain in his love.

(JOHN 15:9-10)

So let us beg forgiveness for all our misdoings, and the wrongs which our Adversary's intervention has moved us to commit. Those who have taken the lead in promoting faction and discord should bethink themselves of that Hope which is common to us all. If men are really living in the fear and love of God, they would sooner endure affliction themselves than see their neighbors suffer, and would prefer reproach to fall on them rather than on the tradition of peaceful harmony which has been so proudly and loyally handed down to us.

Clement of Rome

Love him more

Then Peter came to Jesus and asked, "Lord, how many times shall I forgive my brother when he sins against me? Up to seven times?" Jesus answered, "I tell you, not seven times, but seventy-seven times."
(MATTHEW 18:21-22)

Let there be no brother who has sinned, no matter how seriously, who would look into your eyes seeking forgiveness, and go away without. And should he not seek forgiveness, you should ask him if he wants it. And if after that he were to sin a thousand times, even before your eyes, love him more than me, for this is how you will draw him to the Lord; and always have mercy on such as these.

Francis of Assisi

Forgive, knowing the true value of time

Love does no harm to its neighbor. Therefore
love is the fulfillment of the law. . . .
The night is nearly over; the day is almost here.
So let us put aside the deeds of darkness
and put on the armor of light.
(ROMANS 13:10-12)

A wise man will haste to forgive, because he knows the true value of time, and will not suffer it to pass away in unnecessary pain. . . . Whoever considers the weakness both of himself and others will not long want persuasives to forgiveness. We know not to what degree of malignity any injury is to be imputed, or how much its guilt. . . . We cannot be certain how much more we feel than was intended to be inflicted, or how much we increase the mischief to ourselves by voluntary aggravations. . . . Of him that hopes to be forgiven, it is indispensably required that he forgive. . . . and to him that refuses to practice it, the throne of mercy is inaccessible, and the Saviour of the world has been born in vain.

Samuel Johnson

49.4

Forgiving love at work in us

Be merciful, just as your Father is merciful. Do not judge, and you will not be judged. Do not condemn, and you will not be condemned. Forgive, and you will be forgiven.
(LUKE 6:36-37)

When forgiving love comes to us, it is not only to deliver us from punishment. No, much more; it seeks to win us for its own, to take possession of us and to dwell in us. And when thus it has come down to dwell in us it does not lose its own heavenly character and beauty: it still is forgiving love seeking to do its work, not alone toward us, but in us, and through us, leading and enabling us to forgive those who sin against us. So much so is this the case that we are told that not to forgive is a sure sign that one has himself not been forgiven. He who seeks only forgiveness from selfishness and freedom from punishment, but has not truly accepted forgiving love to rule his heart and life, proves that God's forgiveness has never really reached him.

Andrew Murray

Forgiveness restores
us to family life

If your brother sins, rebuke him, and if he repents, forgive him. If he sins against you seven times in a day, and seven times comes back to you and says, "I repent," forgive him.
(LUKE 17:3-4)

If by *repentance* we mean all that the word means in the New Testament, it will include a forgiving spirit; for to repent is to change one's outlook and to regard men and the world as God regards them. But everyone can feel that the emphasis would be quite different if the words were "Forgive us our trespasses, for we do truly repent of them." This would be like saying, "I am so sorry; and I won't do it again; do forgive me." . . . That is not the basis on which our Lord bids us rest our plea. . . . He is always ready and eager to forgive; but how can he restore us to the freedom and intimacy of the family life if there are other members of the family toward whom we refuse to be friendly?

William Temple

49.6

Restoration—go to the place you lost it

Therefore, if you are offering your gift at the altar and there remember that your brother has something against you, leave your gift there in front of the altar. First go and be reconciled to your brother; then come and offer your gift.

(MATTHEW 5:23-24)

When we set out to seek for anything that we have lost, we do not go gaping about anywhere and everywhere. We go straight to the place where we lost it. . . . On what occasion was it? . . . Was it at that moment when the golden rule leapt too late into your mind? . . . Take up your cross daily in that thing concerning which God has had a controversy with you in your conscience secretly ever since. Was it in that sweet conversation in which you sat and spoke such unanimous things to the depreciation and damage of your brother? If it was . . . go straight to your brother today: or take pen and ink, and tell him that you have not had a dog's life with God ever since.

Alexander Whyte

49.7

WE ARE LIGHT—
SOWERS OF SEED

*For you were once darkness, but now
you are light in the Lord. Live as
children of light (for the fruit of the
light consists in all goodness,
righteousness and truth).*

(EPHESIANS 5:8-9)

Every life an influence

What, after all, is Apollos? And what is Paul?
Only servants, through whom you came
to believe—as the Lord has assigned to each
his task. I planted the seed, Apollos watered it,
but God made it grow. So neither he who
plants nor he who waters is anything,
but only God, who makes things grow.
(1 CORINTHIANS 3:5-7)

All seed-sowing is a mysterious thing, whether the seed fall into the earth or into souls. Man is a husbandman; his whole work rightly understood is to develop life, to show it everywhere. Such is the mission of humanity, and of this divine mission the great instrument is speech. We forget too often that language is both a seed-sowing and a revelation. The influence of a word in season, is it not incalculable? What a mystery is speech! But we are blind to it, because we are carnal and earthly. . . . Every life is a profession of faith and exercises an inevitable and silent propaganda. As far as lies in its power, it tends to transform the universe and humanity into its own image.

Henri-Frédéric Amiel

50.1

Light is for those in darkness

Yet I am writing you a new command;
its truth is seen in him and you, because
the darkness is passing and the true light is
already shining. Anyone who claims to be in
the light but hates his brother is still in the
darkness. Whoever loves his brother lives
in the light, and there is nothing in him
to make him stumble.
(1 JOHN 2:8-10)

A light is always meant for the use of those who are in darkness, that by it they may see. The sun lights up the darkness of this world. A lamp is hung in a room to give it light. The Church of Christ is the light of men. The God of this world hath blinded their eyes (2 Corinthians 4:4). Christ's disciples are to shine into their darkness and give them light. As the rays of light stream forth from the sun and scatter that light all about, so the good works of believers are the light that streams out from them to conquer the surrounding darkness, with its ignorance of God and estrangement from him.

Andrew Murray

50.2

We live to benefit others

*You, my brothers, were called to be free.
But do not use your freedom to indulge the
sinful nature; rather, serve one another in
love. The entire law is summed up in a single
command: "Love your neighbor as yourself."*
(GALATIANS 5:13-14)

We are our best when we try to be it not for ourselves
alone, but for our brethren; and that we take God's
gifts more completely for ourselves when we realize
that he sent them to us for the benefit of other men,
who stand beyond us needing them. . . . If this truth
really took possession of us . . . it would make our
struggles after a higher life so much more intense as
they become more noble. "For their sakes I sanctify
myself," said Jesus; and he hardly ever said words
more wonderful than those. There was the power by
which he was holy; the world was to be made holy,
was to be sanctified through him. I am sure that you
or I could indeed be strengthened to meet some
great experience of pain if we really believed that by
our suffering we were to be made more luminous
with help to other men.

Phillips Brooks

50.3

We must not wait for ideal circumstances

Preach the Word; be prepared in season and out of season; correct, rebuke and encourage—with great patience and careful instruction.
(2 TIMOTHY 4:2)

How searchingly final is the prophet's comment: "He that observeth the wind shall not sow, and he that regardeth the clouds shall not reap." And this trite maxim, a summary of the imperative law of all husbandry, is not just a bit of mere moralizing. It is a positively protective counsel. For a farmer who knows his business does not wait until an ideal day encourages his sowing. Of course he cannot afford to. . . . So, too, our supreme life-duty must be carried on just as wholeheartedly, with just the same faith and courage, when conditions seem unpromising as when prospects flatter. If we wait for ideally favorable weather for the sowing of the good seed, for the investment of our lives in the field of human need and Divine fidelity, we shall die waiting.

J. Stuart Holden

50.4

Placed on a candlestick

Do everything without complaining
or arguing, so that you may become
blameless and pure, children of God without
fault in a crooked and depraved generation,
in which you shine like stars in the universe
as you hold out the word of life.
(PHILIPPIANS 2:14-16)

Your eagerness to mortify yourself should never turn
you from solitude, nor tear you away from external
affairs. You must show yourself and hide yourself in
turn, and speak and be still. God has not placed you
under a bushel, but on a candlestick, so that you may
light all those who are in the house.

Fénelon

Every person a beacon

You are the light of the world. A city on a hill cannot be hidden. Neither do people light a lamp and put it under a bowl. Instead they put it on its stand, and it gives light to everyone in the house. In the same way, let your light shine before men, that they may see your good deeds and praise your Father in heaven.

(MATTHEW 5:14-16)

Thus we all have a cure of souls. Every man is a center of perpetual radiation . . . a beacon which entices a ship upon the rocks if it does not guide it into port. Every man is a priest, even involuntary; his conduct is an unspoken sermon, which is for ever preaching to others. . . . Thence comes the terrible responsibility which weighs upon all. An evil example is a spiritual poison; it is the proclamation of a sacrilegious faith, of an impure God. Sin would be an evil only for him who commits it, were it not a crime toward the weak brethren, whom it corrupts. Therefore it has been said: "It were better for a man not to have been born than to offend one of these little ones."

Henri-Frédéric Amiel

50.6

Wanting to do God's will

*It is God who works in you to will
and to act according to his good purpose.*
(PHILIPPIANS 2:13)

In all the ordinary forms of Christian life, service is apt to have more or less of bondage in it; that is, it is done purely as a matter of duty, and often as a trial and a cross. . . . Now from all these forms of bondage the soul that enters fully into the blessed life of faith is entirely delivered. In the first place, service of any sort becomes delightful to it because, having surrendered its will into the keeping of the Lord, he works in it to will and to do of his good pleasure, and the soul finds itself really wanting to do the things God wants it to do.

Hannah Whitall Smith

BY LOVE CONSTRAINED

*For Christ's love compels us, because we
are convinced that one died for all,
and therefore all died.*

(2 CORINTHIANS 5:14)

51.0

Grace allows us to serve

I thank Christ Jesus our Lord, who has given me strength, that he considered me faithful, appointing me to his service.
(1 TIMOTHY 1:12)

Isaiah 6:8: "Here am I; send me." It is a signal instance of grace on the part of the Lord that I am allowed to be a volunteer. The Lord has a right, a dearly purchased right, to deal with me very differently. He might issue a peremptory command. He might utter his stern voice of authority, and at once, order me. But he knows what is in man better than to treat thus the broken and relenting heart of whom he has smitten by the brightness of his glorious holiness to the ground, and healed by the touch of his ever-living sacrifice of blood. He is considerate. He is generous. His servant is not coerced or constrained, as with a bit and bridle. He has the unspeakable privilege and happiness of giving himself voluntarily . . . to the Lord, who willingly gave himself for him.

Robert S. Candlish

51.1

Willingness to do
anything he asks

*Yet when I preach the gospel, I cannot boast, for
I am compelled to preach. Woe to me if I do not
preach the gospel! If I preach voluntarily, I
have a reward; if not voluntarily, I am simply
discharging the trust committed to me.*

(1 CORINTHIANS 9:16-17)

A . . . thought occurred to my mind that if I was ever
converted I should be obliged to leave my profession, of which I was very fond, and go preaching the
Gospel. This at first stumbled me. I thought I had
taken too much pains, and spent too much time and
study in my profession to think now of becoming a
Christian, if by doing so I should be obliged to
preach the Gospel. However, I at last came to the
conclusion that I must submit that question to God.
But now . . . Nothing, it seemed to me, could be put
in competition with the worth of souls; and no labor
could be so sweet as to be employed in holding up
Christ to a dying world.

Charles G. Finney

51.2

The spirit of missions

Therefore go and make disciples of all nations, baptizing them in the name of the Father and of the Son and of the Holy Spirit, and teaching them to obey everything I have commanded you. And surely I am with you always, to the very end of the age.
(MATTHEW 28:19-20)

The Spirit of Jesus Christ is the spirit of missions. . . . His promise and advent composed the first missionary movement. The missionary . . . movement is the church of Jesus Christ marching in militant array, with the design of possessing the whole world of mankind for Christ. Whoever is touched by the Spirit of God is fired by the missionary spirit. An anti-missionary Christian is a contradiction in terms. . . . Missionary impulse is the heartbeat of our Lord Jesus Christ, sending the vital forces of himself through the whole body of Christ. . . . When these life forces cease, then death ensues. So that anti-missionary churches are dead churches, just as anti-missionary Christians are dead Christians.

E. M. Bounds

51.3

Lift up your neighbor's burden

We urge you, brothers, warn those who are
idle, encourage the timid, help the weak,
be patient with everyone.
(1 THESSALONIANS 5:14)

Our Lord expects works. Therefore when you see anyone sick, have compassion upon her as if she were yourself. Pity her. Fast that she may eat. Wake that she may sleep. Again, when you hear anyone commended in praise, rejoice in it as much as if you were commended and praised yourself. This indeed should be easier, because where true humility is, praise is prompted. Cover also your sister's defects as you would cover and not expose your own defects and faults. As often as an occasion offers, lift up your neighbor's burden. Take it from her heart and put it upon yourself. Satan himself would not be Satan any longer if he could once love his neighbor as himself.

Teresa of Avila

See that the inner life is right

This is to my Father's glory,
that you bear much fruit,
showing yourselves to be my disciples.
(JOHN 15:8)

If you would bear fruit, see that the inner life is perfectly right, that your relation to Christ Jesus is clear and close. Begin each day with him in the morning, to know in truth that you are abiding in him and he in you. Christ tells that nothing less will do. It is not your willing and running, it is not by your might or strength, but—"by my Spirit, saith the Lord." Meet each new engagement, undertake every new work, with an ear and heart open to the Master's voice: "He that abideth in me beareth much fruit."

Andrew Murray

51.5

Believers carry about
their own atmosphere

*But you will receive power when the Holy
Spirit comes on you; and you will be my
witnesses in Jerusalem, and in all Judea
and Samaria, and to the ends of the earth.*
(ACTS 1:8)

In Acts 2, we are told of the fulfillment of [the] promise: "Suddenly out of the heaven a sound as of a rushing violent breath, and it filled the whole house where they were." . . . Is it not this where we often miss the blessing? We narrow down the working of the Spirit of God to the small capacity of the believer, instead of recognizing that God has said that not only may his children be "filled," but *environed* by his Spirit—that those who are born of the Spirit, and joined to him "one spirit" with his beloved Son, shall walk through a world that "lieth in the evil one" carrying about with them their own atmosphere—the very presence of God enveloping them.

Jessie Penn-Lewis

51.6

Come out from the world

Therefore come out from them and
be separate, says the Lord. Touch no
unclean thing,
and I will receive you.
(2 CORINTHIANS 6:17)

The standard of practical holy living has been so low among Christians that the least degree of real devotedness of life and walk is looked upon with surprise and often even with disapprobation by a large portion of the Church. And, for the most part, the followers of the Lord Jesus Christ are satisfied with a life so conformed to the world, and so like it in almost every respect, that, to a casual observer, no difference is discernible. But we who have heard the call of our God to a life of entire consecration and perfect trust must do differently. We must come out from the world and be separate, and must not be conformed to it in our character or in our lives.

Hannah Whitall Smith

INTERCESSION: BE ON SPEAKING TERMS WITH GOD

Therefore confess your sins to each other and pray for each other so that you may be healed. The prayer of a righteous man is powerful and effective.

(JAMES 5:16)

52.0

Power in proportion to prayer

*I know that through your prayers and
the help given by the Spirit of Jesus Christ,
what has happened to me
will turn out for my deliverance.*
(PHILIPPIANS 1:19)

I found myself having more or less power in preaching and in personal labor for souls just in proportion as I had the Spirit of prevailing prayer. I have found that unless I kept myself—or have been kept—in such relation to God as to have daily and hourly access to him in prayer, my efforts to win souls was abortive; but that when I could prevail with God in prayer, I could prevail with man in preaching, exhortation, and conversation.

Charles G. Finney

Prayer enhances our
love for others

And this is my prayer: that your love
may abound more and more
in knowledge and depth of insight.
(PHILIPPIANS 1:9)

There is nothing that makes us love a man so much as praying for him; and when you can once do this sincerely for any man, you have fitted your soul for the performance of everything that is kind and civil toward him. . . . By considering yourself as an advocate with God for your neighbors or acquaintance, you would never find it hard to be at peace with them yourself. It would be easy to you to bear with and forgive those for whom you particularly implored the divine mercy and forgiveness.

William Law

Constrained to pray

*With this in mind, we constantly pray for you,
that our God may count you worthy of his
calling, and that by his power he may fulfill
every good purpose of yours and
every act prompted by your faith.*
(2 Thessalonians 1:11)

I was very strongly exercised in prayer, and had an experience then that was somewhat new to me at the time. I found myself so borne down with the weight of immortal souls that I was constrained to pray . . . and was obliged to retire to the barn frequently through the day, where I could unburden my soul and pour my heart out to God in prayer. . . . When alone I would wrestle and struggle. . . . I would say to God that he had made a promise to answer prayer, and I could not, and would not, be denied. I would be so wrought up as to use such strong language to God in prayer. . . . Frequently I found myself saying to him, "I hope thou dost not think that I can be denied. I come with thy faithful promises in my hand, and I cannot be denied."

Charles G. Finney

52.3

Pray for good and evil people

I urge, then, first of all, that requests, prayers, intercession and thanksgiving be made for everyone—for kings and all those in authority, that we may live peaceful and quiet lives in all godliness and holiness.

(1 TIMOTHY 2:1-2)

Christian lips are to breathe prayers for the cruel and infamous rulers in state as well as for the righteous and the benign governors and princes. . . . All men are to engage our thoughts in approaching a throne of grace. . . . The wants and woes of the entire race are to broaden and make tender our sympathies and inflame our petitions. No little man can pray. No man with narrow views of God, of his plan to save men, and of the universal needs of men, can pray effectually. It takes a broadminded man, who understands God and his purposes in the atonement to pray well. No cynic can pray. Prayer is the divinest philanthropy, as well as giant-great-heartedness. Prayer comes from a big heart, filled with thoughts about men and with sympathies for all men.

E. M. Bounds

52.4

We can yet become
mighty in prayer

*The weapons we fight with are not the weapons
of the world. On the contrary, they have divine
power to demolish strongholds. We demolish
arguments and every pretension that sets itself
up against the knowledge of God,
and we take captive every thought to make
it obedient to Christ.*

(2 CORINTHIANS 10:4-5)

Can it indeed be that those who have never been able
to face, much less to overcome, the difficulty, can yet
become mighty in prayer? Tell me, was it really
possible for Jacob to become Israel—a prince who
prevailed with God? It was. The things that are
impossible with men are possible with God. Have
you not in very deed received from the Father, as the
great fruit of Christ's redemption, the spirit of supplication, the spirit of intercession? Just pause and
think what that means. . . . Oh, let us banish all fear,
and in faith claim the grace for which we have the
Holy Spirit dwelling in us, the grace of supplication,
the grace of intercession.

Andrew Murray

52.5

Intercession: Our first work

Give ear to my words, O LORD, consider my sighing. Listen to my cry for help, my King and my God, for to you I pray. In the morning, O LORD, you hear my voice; in the morning I lay my requests before you and wait in expectation.

(PSALM 5:1-3)

In all his instructions, our Lord Jesus spoke much oftener to his disciples about their praying than their preaching. In the farewell discourse he said little about preaching, but much about the Holy Spirit, and their asking whatsoever they would in his Name. If we are to return to this life of the first apostles and of Paul, and really accept the truth every day—my first work, my only strength, is intercession, to secure the power of God on the souls entrusted to me—we must have the courage to confess past sin, and to believe that there is deliverance.

Andrew Murray

Show by our forbearance
we are brothers

Pray for the happiness of those who curse you;
implore God's blessing on those who hurt you.
(LUKE 6:28, TLB)

Regarding the rest of mankind, you should pray for
them unceasingly, for we can always hope that repentance may enable them to find their way to God.
Give them a chance to learn from you, or at all
events from the way you act. Meet their animosity
with mildness, their high words with humility, and
their abuse with your prayers. But stand firm against
their errors, and if they grow violent, be gentle
instead of wanting to pay them back in their own
coin. Let us show by our forbearance that we are
their brothers, and try to imitate the Lord by seeing
which of us can put up with the most ill-usage or
privation of contempt—so that in this way none of
the devil's noxious weeds may take root among you,
but you may rest in Jesus Christ in all sanctity and
discipline of body and soul.

Ignatius of Antioch

52.7

Sources

1.1 Robert Murray McCheyne, *Memoirs and Remains of Robert Murray McCheyne,* quoted in *Giant Steps,* ed. Warren W. Wiersbe (Grand Rapids: Baker, 1981), 102-103.

1.2 F. B. Meyer, "Frederick Brotherton Meyer," quoted in *Giant Steps,* ed. Warren W. Wiersbe (Grand Rapids: Baker, 1981), 228.

1.3 Teresa of Avila, *A Life of Prayer* (Portland, Oreg.: Multnomah, 1983), 145.

1.4 Barnabas, The Epistle of Barnabas, in *Early Christian Writings* (New York: Dorset Press, 1986), 217.

1.5 A. W. Tozer, *The Knowledge of the Holy* (New York: Harper & Row, 1961), 49-50.

1.6 John Owen, *Thinking Spiritually* (London: Grace Publications, 1989), 25.

1.7 Teresa of Avila, *A Life of Prayer* (Portland, Oreg.: Multnomah, 1983), 142.

2.1 Robert Murray McCheyne, *Memoirs and Remains of Robert Murray McCheyne,* quoted in *Giant Steps,* ed. Warren W. Wiersbe (Grand Rapids: Baker, 1981), 100.

2.2 John Owen, *Thinking Spiritually* (London: Grace Publications, 1989), 37.

2.3 Jeanne Guyon, *Experiencing God through Prayer* (Springdale, Pa.: Whitaker House, n.d.), 25.

2.4 Thomas Manton, *An Exposition of John XVII*, quoted in *Giant Steps*, ed. Warren W. Wiersbe (Grand Rapids: Baker, 1981), 27.

2.5 Thomas R. Kelly, *A Testament of Devotion* (New York: Harper & Row, 1941), 352.

2.6 Thomas Manton, *An Exposition of John XVII*, quoted in *Giant Steps*, ed. Warren W. Wiersbe (Grand Rapids: Baker, 1981), 28.

2.7 Ignatius of Antioch, Epistle to the Magnesians, in *Early Christian Writings* (New York: Dorset Press, 1986), 88.

3.1 A. W. Tozer, *The Pursuit of God* (Harrisburg, Pa.: Christian Publications, 1948), 65.

3.2 Ibid.

3.3 A. W. Tozer, *The Knowledge of the Holy* (New York: Harper & Row, 1961), 76-77.

3.4 Barnabas, The Epistle of Barnabas, in *Early Christian Writings* (New York: Dorset Press, 1986), 202.

3.5 J. P. de Caussade, "Dominus Est," in *A Diary*

of Readings, ed. John Baillie (1955; reprint, New York: Macmillan, 1986), day 78.

3.6 Martin Luther, "Table-talk," in *A Diary of Readings,* ed. John Baillie (1955; reprint, New York: Macmillan, 1986), day 353.

3.7 Hannah Whitall Smith, *The Christian's Secret of a Happy Life* (Old Tappan, N.J.: Revell, 1952), 220.

4.1 Charles G. Finney, *Memoirs of Charles G. Finney* (Grand Rapids: Zondervan, 1989), 39.

4.2 Teresa of Avila, *A Life of Prayer* (Portland, Oreg.: Multnomah, 1983), 215.

4.3 Augustine of Hippo, *The Confessions of St. Augustine,* trans. Edward Pusey (New York: Pocket Books, 1951), 195.

4.4 Hannah Whitall Smith, *The Christian's Secret of a Happy Life* (Old Tappan, N.J.: Revell, 1952), 92–93.

4.5 A. W. Tozer, *The Pursuit of God* (Harrisburg, Pa.: Christian Publications, 1948), 15.

4.6 Richard Baxter, "Why We Should Think about God," in *A Diary of Readings,* ed. John Baillie (1955; reprint, New York: Macmillan, 1986), day 310.

4.7 Alexander Maclaren, *Expositions of Holy*

Scripture, quoted in *Giant Steps,* ed. Warren W. Wiersbe (Grand Rapids: Baker, 1981), 148.

5.1 Andrew Murray, *Like Christ,* in *The Best of Andrew Murray* (Grand Rapids: Baker, 1990), 32.

5.2 Andrew Murray, *The True Vine* (Chicago: Moody Press, n.d.), 11.

5.3 Andrew Murray, "Like Christ: In His Dependence on the Father," in *The Best of Andrew Murray* (Grand Rapids: Baker, 1990), 42–43.

5.4 Andrew Murray, *The True Vine* (Chicago: Moody Press, n.d.), 13.

5.5 Jeanne Guyon, *Madame Guyon, an Autobiography* (Chicago: Moody Press, n.d.), 14.

5.6 Andrew Murray, *The True Vine* (Chicago: Moody Press, n.d.), 82.

5.7 Oswald Chambers, *Making All Things New* (Oswald Chambers Publications Association, Ltd., 1930), 30–31.

6.1 A. W. Tozer, *The Pursuit of God* (Harrisburg, Pa.: Christian Publications, 1948), 91.

6.2 John Owen, *Thinking Spiritually* (London: Grace Publications, 1989), 18.

6.3 Jessie Penn-Lewis, *Power for Service* (Bristol, England: Overcomer Publications, n.d.), 23.

6.4 Oswald Chambers, *Making All Things New*

(Oswald Chambers Publications Association, Ltd., 1930), 51.

6.5 François Fénelon, *Christian Perfection* (New York: Harper & Row, 1947), 53.

6.6 Francis Paget, "The Vacant Heart," in *A Diary of Readings*, ed. John Baillie (1955; reprint, New York: Macmillan, 1986), day 164.

6.7 Thomas Traherne, *Centuries* (Wilton, Conn.: Morehouse-Barlow, 1986), 134.

7.1 Jeanne Guyon, *Experiencing God through Prayer* (Springdale, Pa.: Whitaker House, 1984), 41.

7.2 Thomas Traherne, *Centuries* (Wilton, Conn.: Morehouse-Barlow, 1986), 17.

7.3 Martyn Lloyd-Jones, *God's Ultimate Purpose*, quoted in *Giant Steps*, ed. Warren W. Wiersbe (Grand Rapids: Baker, 1981), 365.

7.4 Mrs. Pearsall Smith, "Knowledge by Acquaintance," in *A Diary of Readings*, ed. John Baillie (1955; reprint, New York: Macmillan, 1986), day 254.

7.5 John Newton, *The Letters of John Newton*, quoted in *Giant Steps*, ed. Warren W. Wiersbe (Grand Rapids: Baker, 1981), 67.

7.6 Sir Arthur Eddington, "The Security We Desire," in *A Diary of Readings*, ed. John Baillie

(1955; reprint, New York: Macmillan, 1986), day
260.

7.7 Andrew Murray, *The True Vine* (Chicago:
Moody Press, n.d.), 113–114.

8.1 Jeanne Guyon, *Madame Guyon, an
Autobiography* (Chicago: Moody Press, n.d.),
72–73.

8.2 A. W. Tozer, *The Pursuit of God* (Harrisburg,
Pa.: Christian Publications, 1948), 71.

8.3 Forbes Robinson, "On Being Alone," in *A
Diary of Readings,* ed. John Baillie (1955; reprint,
New York: Macmillan, 1986), day 262.

8.4 Lorenzo Scupoli, "The Spiritual Combat," in
A Diary of Readings, ed. John Baillie (1955;
reprint, New York: Macmillan, 1986), day 214.

8.5 Jeanne Guyon, *Madame Guyon, an
Autobiography* (Chicago: Moody Press, n.d.), 16.

8.6 Anselm, "The Goodness of God," in *A Diary
of Readings,* ed. John Baillie (1955; reprint, New
York: Macmillan, 1986), day 332.

8.7 Hannah Whitall Smith, *The Christian's Secret
of a Happy Life* (Old Tappan, N.J.: Revell, 1952),
67.

9.1 John Newton, "What Happens to Our
Plans,"in *A Diary of Readings,* ed. John Baillie

(1955; reprint, New York: Macmillan, 1986), day 186.

9.2 Jessie Penn-Lewis, *Power for Service* (Bristol, England: Overcomer Publications, n.d.), 6.

9.3 F. B. Meyer, quoted in *Giant Steps,* ed. Warren W. Wiersbe (Grand Rapids: Baker, 1981), 224.

9.4 A. W. Tozer, *The Divine Conquest,* quoted in *Giant Steps,* ed. Warren W. Wiersbe (Grand Rapids: Baker, 1981), 354–355.

9.5 François Fénelon, *Christian Perfection* (New York: Harper & Row, 1947), 156.

9.6 John Newton, *The Letters of John Newton,* quoted in *Giant Steps,* ed. Warren W. Wiersbe (Grand Rapids: Baker, 1981), 68.

9.7 Charles G. Finney, *Memoirs of Charles G. Finney* (Grand Rapids: Zondervan, 1989), 39.

10.1 J. Stuart Holden, *A Voice of God,* quoted in *Giant Steps,* ed. Warren W. Wiersbe (Grand Rapids: Baker, 1981), 323.

10.2 Andrew Murray, "Holiness and Happiness," in *The Best of Andrew Murray* (Grand Rapids: Baker, 1990), 82.

10.3 Jessie Penn-Lewis, *Power for Service* (Bristol, England: Overcomer Publications, n.d.), 29.

10.4 Ibid., 11.1

10.5 Henry Drummond, "God's Business," in *A Diary of Readings,* ed. John Baillie (1955; reprint, New York: Macmillan, 1986), day 215.

10.6 E. M. Bounds, *The Essentials of Prayer,* in *The Complete Works of E. M. Bounds* (Grand Rapids: Baker, 1990), 131–132.

10.7 Jessie Penn-Lewis, *Power for Service* (Bristol, England: Overcomer Publications, n.d.), 45.

11.1 Oswald Chambers, *Making All Things New* (Oswald Chambers Publications Association, Ltd., 1930), 73.

11.2 Oswald Chambers, *Bringing Sons into Glory* (Oswald Chambers Publications Association, Ltd., 1943), 116.

11.3 Ibid., 42–43.

11.4 Oswald Chambers, *Making All Things New* (Oswald Chambers Publications Association, Ltd., 1930), 73.

11.5 Dietrich Bonhoeffer, *Letters and Papers from Prison,* rev. ed. (New York: Scribner, 1972), 5.

11.6 Lesslie Newbigin, "The Christian Motive," in *A Diary of Readings,* ed. John Baillie (1955; reprint, New York: Macmillan, 1986), day 327.

11.7 Oswald Chambers, *My Utmost for His*

Highest, quoted in *Giant Steps,* ed. Warren W. Wiersbe (Grand Rapids: Baker, 1981), 316.

12.1 François Fénelon, *Christian Perfection* (New York: Harper & Row, 1947), 10–11.

12.2 Jeanne Guyon, *Experiencing God through Prayer* (Springdale, Pa.: Whitaker House, 1984), 17.

12.3 Andrew Murray, "Meditation," in *The Best of Andrew Murray* (Grand Rapids: Baker, 1990), 173.

12.4 François Fénelon, *Christian Perfection* (New York: Harper & Row, 1947), 44.

12.5 Richard Baxter, "Where to meditate," in *A Diary of Readings,* ed. John Baillie (1955; reprint, New York: Macmillan, 1986), day 20.

12.6 Forbes Robinson, "On Being Alone," in *A Diary of Readings,* ed. John Baillie (1955; reprint, New York: Macmillan, 1986), day 262.

12.7 Augustine of Hippo, *The Confessions of St. Augustine,* trans. Edward Pusey (New York: Pocket Books, 1951), 217.

13.1 François Malaval, "Spiritual Dryness," in *A Diary of Readings,* ed. John Baillie (1955; reprint, New York: Macmillan, 1986), day 346.

13.2 E. M. Bounds, *The Necessity of Prayer,* in *The Complete Works of E. M. Bounds* (Grand Rapids: Baker, 1990), 30.

13.3 Thomas Traherne, *Centuries* (Wilton, Conn.: Morehouse-Barlow, 1986), 5.

13.4 Philip Doddridge, *The Rise and Progress of Religion in the Soul,* quoted in *Giant Steps,* ed. Warren W. Wiersbe (Grand Rapids: Baker, 1981), 48–49.

13.5 James Martineau, "Of Silent Meditation," in *A Diary of Readings,* ed. John Baillie (1955; reprint, New York: Macmillan, 1986), day 246.

13.6 John Owen, *Thinking Spiritually* (London, England: Grace Publications, 1989), 38.

13.7 Augustine of Hippo, "Christians and the Sack of Rome," in *A Diary of Readings,* ed. John Baillie (1955; reprint, New York: Macmillan, 1986), day 170.

14.1 Andrew Murray, "Like Christ: In His Use of Scripture," in *The Best of Andrew Murray* (Grand Rapids: Baker, 1990), 46.

14.2 John Calvin, *Institutes of the Christian Religion,* quoted in *Giant Steps,* ed. Warren W. Wiersbe (Grand Rapids: Baker, 1981), 48–49.

14.3 Andrew Murray, "Meditation," in *The Best of Andrew Murray* (Grand Rapids: Baker, 1990), 173.

14.4 Martin Luther, "The Law and the Gospel," in *A Diary of Readings,* ed. John Baillie (1955; reprint, New York: Macmillan, 1986), day 306.

14.5 Ignatius of Antioch, *Letter to the Ephesians,* in *Early Christian Writings* (New York: Dorset Press, 1986), 80.

14.6 James Stalker, *The Four Men,* quoted in *Giant Steps,* ed. Warren W. Wiersbe (Grand Rapids: Baker, 1981), 48–49.

14.7 Martin Luther, Sermon on John 6–8, in *Day by Day We Magnify Thee* (Minneapolis: Fortress Press, 1982), 107.

15.1 Charles G. Finney, *Memoirs of Charles G. Finney* (Grand Rapids: Zondervan, 1989), 139.

15.2 Thomas Traherne, *Centuries* (Wilton, Conn.: Morehouse-Barlow, 1986), 20.

15.3 Martin Luther, "Our Feelings and Our Faith," in *A Diary of Readings,* ed. John Baillie (1955; reprint, New York: Macmillan, 1986), day 340.

15.4 John Bunyan, quoted in *Giant Steps,* ed. Warren W. Wiersbe (Grand Rapids: Baker, 1981), 34.

15.5 Martin Luther, "The Definition of Christ," in *A Diary of Readings,* ed. John Baillie (1955; reprint, New York: Macmillan, 1986), day 135.

15.6 Thomas à Kempis, *The Imitation of Christ,* quoted in *Giant Steps,* ed. Warren W. Wiersbe (Grand Rapids: Baker, 1981), 15.

15.7 Martin Luther, Exposition of Genesis 3, in *Day by Day We Magnify Thee* (Minneapolis: Fortress Press, 1982), 109.

16.1 E. M. Bounds, *The Reality of Prayer,* in *The Complete Works of E. M. Bounds* (Grand Rapids: Baker, 1990), 231.

16.2 John Calvin, *Institutes of the Christian Religion,* quoted in *Giant Steps,* ed. Warren W. Wiersbe (Grand Rapids: Baker, 1981), 19.

16.3 E. M. Bounds, *Power through Prayer,* in *The Complete Works of E. M. Bounds* (Grand Rapids: Baker, 1990), 464.

16.4 E. M. Bounds, *The Weapon of Prayer,* in *The Complete Works of E. M. Bounds* (Grand Rapids: Baker, 1990), 371.

16.5 E. M. Bounds, *The Reality of Prayer,* in *The Complete Works of E. M. Bounds* (Grand Rapids: Baker, 1990), 226.

16.6 E. M. Bounds, *The Possibilities of Prayer,* in *The Complete Works of E. M. Bounds* (Grand Rapids: Baker, 1990), 339.

16.7 William Law, *A Serious Call to a Devout and Holy Life* (E. P. Dutton, 1906), 162–163.

17.1 E. M. Bounds, *The Necessity of Prayer,* in *The Complete Works of E. M. Bounds* (Grand Rapids: Baker, 1990), 49.

17.2 John Owen, *Thinking Spiritually,* (London: Grace Publications, 1989), 67.

17.3 Andrew Murray, "Prayer in Harmony with God," in *The Best of Andrew Murray* (Grand Rapids: Baker, 1990), 26.

17.4 E. M. Bounds, *The Weapon of Prayer,* in *The Complete Works of E. M. Bounds* (Grand Rapids: Baker, 1990), 371.

17.5 E. M. Bounds, *The Necessity of Prayer,* in *The Complete Works of E. M. Bounds* (Grand Rapids: Baker, 1990), 61.

17.6 John Owen, *Thinking Spiritually* (London: Grace Publications, 1989), 50.

17.7 Ibid., 14.

18.1 E. M. Bounds, *The Possibilities of Prayer,* in *The Complete Works of E. M. Bounds* (Grand Rapids: Baker, 1990), 164.

18.2 E. M. Bounds, *The Necessity of Prayer,* in *The Complete Works of E. M. Bounds* (Grand Rapids: Baker, 1990), 31.

18.3 Teresa of Avila, *A Life of Prayer* (Portland, Oreg.: Multnomah, 1983), 122.

18.4 Ibid., 120.

18.5 Andrew Murray, "The Power of Persevering

Prayer," in *The Best of Andrew Murray* (Grand Rapids: Baker, 1990), 18.

18.6 Jeanne Guyon, *Madame Guyon, an Autobiography* (Chicago: Moody Press, n.d.), 46–47.

18.7 E. M. Bounds, *The Purpose in Prayer,* in *The Complete Works of E. M. Bounds* (Grand Rapids: Baker, 1990), 343.

19.1 E. M. Bounds, *The Possibilities of Prayer,* in *The Complete Works of E. M. Bounds* (Grand Rapids: Baker, 1990), 153.

19.2 Ibid., 190.

19.3 Ibid., 162.

19.4 John Owen, *Thinking Spiritually* (London: Grace Publications, 1989), 51.

19.5 Ibid., 52.

19.6 Ibid., 57.

19.7 Ibid., 59.

20.1 Søren Kierkegaard, "In the Name of Jesus," in *A Diary of Readings,* ed. John Baillie (1955; reprint, New York: Macmillan, 1986), day 21.

20.2 François Fénelon, *Christian Perfection* (New York: Harper & Row, 1947), 10.

20.3 Jeanne Guyon, *Madame Guyon, an Autobiography* (Chicago: Moody Press, n.d.), 103.

20.4 Ibid., 156.

20.5 François Fénelon, *Christian Perfection* (New York: Harper & Row, 1947), 154.

20.6 Thomas Chalmers, "What Meaneth this Restlessness?" in *A Diary of Readings,* ed. John Baillie (1955; reprint, New York: Macmillan, 1986), day 309.

20.7 Martin Luther, Sermons from the Year 1527, in *Day by Day We Magnify Thee* (Minneapolis: Fortress Press, 1982), 343.

21.1 Alexander Whyte in *Giant Steps,* ed. Warren W. Wiersbe (Grand Rapids: Baker, 1981), 202.

21.2 Charles G. Finney, *Memoirs of Charles G. Finney* (Grand Rapids: Zondervan, 1989), 139.

21.3 Andrew Murray, "In the Name of Christ," in *The Best of Andrew Murray* (Grand Rapids: Baker, 1990), 117.

21.4 Andrew Murray, "The Power of Persevering Prayer," in *The Best of Andrew Murray* (Grand Rapids: Baker, 1990), 20.

21.5 E. M. Bounds, *The Essentials of Prayer,* in *The Complete Works of E. M. Bounds* (Grand Rapids: Baker, 1990), 106.

21.6 Francis de Sales, "When Consolation Fails," in *A Diary of Readings*, ed. John Baillie (1955; reprint, New York: Macmillan, 1986), day 217.

21.7 Martin Luther, Exposition of Four Comforting, in *Day by Day We Magnify Thee* (Minneapolis: Fortress Press, 1982), 320.

22.1 Thomas à Kempis, "Few Bearers of His Cross," in *A Diary of Readings*, ed. John Baillie (1955; reprint, New York: Macmillan, 1986), day 190.

22.2 François Fénelon, *Christian Perfection* (New York: Harper & Row, 1947), 21.

22.3 Philip Doddridge, *The Rise and Progress of Religion in the Soul*, quoted in *Giant Steps*, ed. Warren W. Wiersbe (Grand Rapids: Baker, 1981), 47.

22.4 Dietrich Bonhoeffer, *Letters and Papers from Prison*, rev. ed. (New York: Collier Books, 1972), 13.

22.5 Ignatius of Antioch, Epistle to the Romans, in *Early Christian Writings* (New York: Dorset Press, 1986), 105–106.

22.6 Dietrich Bonhoeffer, *Letters and Papers from Prison*, rev. ed. (New York: Collier Books, 1972), 14.

22.7 François Fénelon, *Christian Perfection* (New York: Harper & Row, 1947), 25.

23.1 Jean Nicolas Grou, "Praying for Humility," in *A Diary of Readings,* ed. John Baillie (1955; reprint, New York: Macmillan, 1986), day 29.

23.2 John Bunyan, quoted in *Giant Steps,* ed. Warren W. Wiersbe (Grand Rapids: Baker, 1981), 36.

23.3 A. W. Tozer, *That Incredible Christian* (Harrisburg, Pa.: Christian Publications, 1964), 11–12.

23.4 Augustine of Hippo, "Christians and the Sack of Rome," in *A Diary of Readings,* ed. John Baillie (1955; reprint, New York: Macmillan, 1986), day 170.

23.5 Dietrich Bonhoeffer, *Letters and Papers from Prison,* rev. ed. (New York: Collier Books, 1972), 14.

23.6 A. W. Tozer, *The Pursuit of God* (Harrisburg, Pa.: Christian Publications, 1948), 57.

23.7 Martin Luther, Sermon on the Third Sunday After Trinity, 1544, in *Day by Day We Magnify Thee* (Minneapolis: Fortress Press, 1982), 386.

24.1 Baron Friedrich von Hügel, "Sulking through the Inevitable," in *A Diary of Readings,* ed. John Baillie (1955; reprint, New York: Macmillan, 1986), day 162.

24.2 François Fénelon, *Christian Perfection* (New York: Harper & Row, 1947), 66.

24.3 G. Campbell Morgan, *The Westminster Pulpit,* in *Giant Steps,* ed. Warren W. Wiersbe (Grand Rapids: Baker, 1981), 269.

24.4 E. M. Bounds, *The Essentials of Prayer,* in *The Complete Works of E. M. Bounds* (Grand Rapids: Baker, 1990), 109.

24.5 François Fénelon, *Christian Perfection* (New York: Harper & Row, 1947), 170.

24.6 Andrew A. Bonar, *Diary and Letters,* in *Giant Steps,* ed. Warren W. Wiersbe (Grand Rapids: Baker, 1981), 95–96.

24.7 Martin Luther, Sermon on Suffering and the Cross, in *Day by Day We Magnify Thee* (Fortress Press, 1982), 118.

25.1 Henri de Tourville, "God Loves Us," in *A Diary of Readings,* ed. John Baillie (1955; reprint, New York: Macmillan, 1986), day 328.

25.2 François Fénelon, *Christian Perfection* (New York: Harper & Row, 1947), 54–55.

25.3 Thomas Traherne, *Centuries* (Wilton, Conn.: Morehouse-Barlow, 1986), 131.

25.4 Andrew Murray, "Abide in Christ, All Ye Who Have Come to Him," in *The Best of Andrew Murray* (Grand Rapids: Baker, 1990), 55–56.

25.5 Clement of Rome, in *Early Christian Writings* (New York: Dorset Press, 1986), 54.

25.6 Daniel Steele, *Love Enthroned* (New York: Eaton and Mains, 1902), 24.

25.7 Andrew Murray, *The True Vine* (Chicago: Moody Press, n.d.), 78–79.

26.1 Anselm, "The Manhood of Christ," in *A Diary of Readings,* ed. John Baillie (1955; reprint, New York: Macmillan, 1986), day 222.

26.2 John of Ruysbroeck, "The Fruits of Humility," in *A Diary of Readings,* ed. John Baillie (1955; reprint, New York: Macmillan, 1986), day 221.

26.3 François Fénelon, *Christian Perfection* (New York: Harper & Row, 1947), 30.

26.4 Ibid., 34.

26.5 Max Müller, "That Ye Love One Another," in *A Diary of Readings,* ed. John Baillie (1955; reprint, New York: Macmillan, 1986), day 361.

26.6 Ignatius of Antioch, Letter to the Ephesians, in *Early Christian Writings* (New York: Dorset Press, 1986), 77.

26.7 François Fénelon, *Christian Perfection* (New York: Harper & Row, 1947), 9.

27.1 Gregory Dix, "Throughout All Ages," in *A Diary of Readings,* ed. John Baillie (1955; reprint, New York: Macmillan, 1986), day 64.

27.2 François Fénelon, *Christian Perfection* (New York: Harper & Row, 1947), 27.

27.3 Ibid., 38.

27.4 Herbert Henry Farmer, *Things Not Seen: Studies in the Christian Interpretation of Life,* quoted in *Giant Steps,* ed. Warren W. Wiersbe (Grand Rapids: Baker, 1981), 345–346.

27.5 François Fénelon, *Christian Perfection* (New York: Harper & Row, 1947), 37.

27.6 Thomas Chalmers, "The Demand and the Doctrine," in *A Diary of Readings,* ed. John Baillie (1955; reprint, New York: Macmillan, 1986), day 336.

27.7 Robert Murray McCheyne, *Memoirs and Remains of Robert Murray McCheyne,* quoted in *Giant Steps,* ed. Warren W. Wiersbe (Grand Rapids: Baker, 1981), 98–99.

28.1 François Fénelon, *Christian Perfection* (New York: Harper & Row, 1947), 22.

28.2 John Tillotson, "The Inward Tribunal," in

A Diary of Readings, ed. John Baillie (1955; reprint, New York: Macmillan, 1986), day 201.

28.3 Andrew Murray, "On Learning Obedience," in *The Best of Andrew Murray* (Grand Rapids: Baker, 1990), 135.

28.4 François Fénelon, *Christian Perfection* (New York: Harper & Row, 1947), 34.

28.5 E. M. Bounds, *The Necessity of Prayer,* in *The Complete Works of E. M. Bounds* (Grand Rapids: Baker, 1990), 48.

28.6 W. H. Griffith Thomas, *Studies in Colossians and Philemon,* quoted in *Giant Steps,* ed. Warren W. Wiersbe (Grand Rapids: Baker, 1981), 260.

28.7 François Fénelon, *Christian Perfection* (New York: Harper & Row, 1947), 7.

29.1 Frederick William Faber, "Hidden Corners," in *A Diary of Readings,* ed. John Baillie (1955; reprint, New York: Macmillan, 1986), day 233.

29.2 Thomas à Kempis, "The Peaceable Man," in *A Diary of Readings,* ed. John Baillie (1955; reprint, New York: Macmillan, 1986), day 355.

29.3 François Fénelon, *Christian Perfection* (New York: Harper & Row, 1947), 36.

29.4 Ibid., 4.

29.5 A. W. Tozer, *The Pursuit of God* (Harrisburg, Pa.: Christian Publications, 1948), 44.

29.6 Jeanne Guyon, *Experiencing God through Prayer* (Springdale, Pa.: Whitaker House, 1984), 51–52.

29.7 Frederick W. Robertson, in *Giant Steps,* ed. Warren W. Wiersbe (Grand Rapids: Baker, 1981), 115–116.

30.1 Thomas à Kempis, "The Peaceable Man," in *A Diary of Readings,* ed. John Baillie (1955; reprint, New York: Macmillan, 1986), day 355.

30.2 John Henry Newman, *Parochial and Plain Sermons,* quoted in *Giant Steps,* ed. Warren W. Wiersbe, (Grand Rapids: Baker, 1981), 84–85.

30.3 Charles G. Finney, *Memoirs of Charles G. Finney* (Grand Rapids, Zondervan, 1989), 39.

30.4 François Fénelon, *Christian Perfection* (New York: Harper & Row, 1947), 57–58.

30.5 Ibid., 8.

30.6 George Macdonald, *Life Essential: The Hope of the Gospel,* quoted in *Giant Steps,* ed. Warren W. Wiersbe (Grand Rapids: Baker, 1981), 140.

30.7 John Calvin, *Institutes of the Christian Religion,* quoted in *Giant Steps,* ed. Warren W. Wiersbe (Grand Rapids: Baker, 1981), 22–23.

31.1 Charles G. Finney, *Memoirs of Charles G. Finney* (Grand Rapids: Zondervan, 1989), 330.

31.2 A. W. Tozer, *The Pursuit of God* (Harrisburg, Pa.: Christian Publications, 1948), 104.

31.3 Barnabas, The Epistle of Barnabas, in *Early Christian Writings* (New York: Dorset Press, 1986), 196.

31.4 William Law, *A Serious Call to a Devout and Holy Life* (E. P. Dutton, 1906), 119–120.

31.5 François Fénelon, *Christian Perfection* (New York: Harper & Row, 1947), 3.

31.6 F. J. A. Hort, "Our Inconsistencies," in *A Diary of Readings,* ed. John Baillie (1955; reprint, New York: Macmillan, 1986), day 74.

31.7 François Fénelon, *Christian Perfection* (New York: Harper & Row, 1947), 151.

32.1 E. M. Bounds, *The Necessity of Prayer,* in *The Complete Works of E. M. Bounds* (Grand Rapids: Baker, 1990), 58.

32.2 Barnabas, The Epistle of Barnabas, in *Early Christian Writings* (New York: Dorset Press, 1986), 218–219.

32.3 William Law, *A Serious Call to a Devout and Holy Life* (E. P. Dutton, 1906), 17.

32.4 A. W. Tozer, *The Pursuit of God* (Harrisburg, Pa.: Christian Publications, 1948), 28.

32.5 Max Müller, "God's Lendings," in *A Diary of Readings,* ed. John Baillie (1955; reprint, New York: Macmillan, 1986), day 124.

32.6 George Macdonald, *Life Essential: The Hope of the Gospel,* quoted in *Giant Steps,* ed. Warren W. Wiersbe (Grand Rapids: Baker, 1981), 142–143.

32.7 William Penn, "Of Murmuring," in *A Diary of Readings,* ed. John Baillie (1955; reprint, New York: Macmillan, 1986), day 83.

33.1 William Law, *A Serious Call to a Devout and Holy Life* (E. P. Dutton, 1908), 7.

33.2 Ibid., 51.

33.3 Ibid., 54.

33.4 Brother Giles, "The Way of Blessedness," in *A Diary of Readings,* ed. John Baillie (1955; reprint, New York: Macmillan, 1986), day 236.

33.5 John Bunyan, *The Saint's Knowledge of Christ's Love,* quoted in *Giant Steps,* ed. Warren W. Wiersbe (Grand Rapids: Baker, 1981), 35.

33.6 Augustine of Hippo, *The Confessions of St. Augustine,* trans. Edward Pusey (New York: Pocket Books, 1951), 12.

33.7 Jeanne Guyon, *Madame Guyon, an Autobiography* (Chicago: Moody Press, n.d.), 14.

34.1 Dwight L. Moody, *The Best of Dwight L. Moody,* quoted in *Giant Steps,* ed. Warren W. Wiersbe (Grand Rapids: Baker, 1981), 210.

34.2 John Owen, *Thinking Spiritually* (London: Grace Publications, 1989), 30–31.

34.3 Ibid., 29-30.

34.4 T. M. Taylor, "Life is Paradoxical," in *A Diary of Readings,* ed. John Baillie (1955; reprint, New York: Macmillan, 1986), day 116.

34.5 A. W. Tozer, *The Pursuit of God* (Harrisburg, Pa.: Christian Publications, 1948), 19.

34.6 Bernard of Clairvaux, "Seek Ye First . . . ," in *A Diary of Readings,* ed. John Baillie (1955; reprint, New York: Macmillan, 1986), day 56.

34.7 Thomas à Kempis, "The Peaceable Man," in *A Diary of Readings,* ed. John Baillie (1955; reprint, New York: Macmillan, 1986), day 355.

35.1 J. Hudson Taylor, *Hudson Taylor's Legacy,* quoted in *Giant Steps,* ed. Warren W. Wiersbe (Grand Rapids: Baker, 1981), 176–177.

35.2 John Owen, *Thinking Spiritually* (London: Grace Publications, 1989), 47.

35.3 John Newton, "One Branch of Blessedness,"

in *A Diary of Readings,* ed. John Baillie (1955; reprint, New York: Macmillan, 1986), day 329.

35.4 François Fénelon, *Christian Perfection* (New York: Harper & Row, 1947), 7.

35.5 Robert S. Candlish, *Sermons by the Late Robert Candlish,* quoted in *Giant Steps,* ed. Warren W. Wiersbe (Grand Rapids: Baker, 1981), 89–90.

35.6 John Wesley, "John Wesley's Heart Strangely Warmed," in *A Diary of Readings,* ed. John Baillie (1955; reprint, New York: Macmillan, 1986), day 73.

35.7 W. M. MacGregor, "Sometimes to be Reckless," in *A Diary of Readings,* ed. John Baillie (1955; reprint, New York: Macmillan, 1986), day 80.

36.1 Phillips Brooks, *Sermons,* quoted in *Giant Steps,* ed. Warren W. Wiersbe (Grand Rapids: Baker, 1981), 196.

36.2 E. M. Bounds, *The Essentials of Prayer,* in *The Complete Works of E. M. Bounds* (Grand Rapids: Baker, 1990), 94.

36.3 François Fénelon, *Christian Perfection* (New York: Harper & Row, 1947), 21.

36.4 Andrew Murray, "Holiness and Happiness," in *The Best of Andrew Murray* (Grand Rapids: Baker, 1998), 85–86.

36.5 John Wesley, *The Works of John Wesley,* quoted in *Giant Steps,* ed. Warren W. Wiersbe (Grand Rapids: Baker, 1981), 54.

36.6 Philip Doddridge, *The Rise and Progress of Religion in the Soul,* quoted in *Giant Steps,* ed. Warren W. Wiersbe (Grand Rapids: Baker, 1981), 46.

36.7 Martin Luther, "The Enslaved Will," in *Day by Day We Magnify Thee* (Minneapolis: Fortress Press, 1982), 327.

37.1 Oswald Chambers, *Making All Things New* (Oswald Chambers Publications Association, Ltd., 1930), 23–24.

37.2 Clement of Rome, in *Early Christian Writings* (New York: Dorset Press, 1986), 49–50.

37.3 Thomas à Kempis, *The Imitation of Christ,* quoted in *Giant Steps,* ed. Warren W. Wiersbe (Grand Rapids: Baker, 1981), 12.

37.4 Teresa of Avila, *A Life of Prayer* (Portland, Oreg.: Multnomah, 1983), 122.

37.5 François Fénelon, *Christian Perfection* (New York: Harper & Row, 1947), 68.

37.6 Ibid., 90.

37.7 Dietrich Bonhoeffer, "Absolute Truthfulness," in *A Diary of Readings,* ed. John

Baillie (1955; reprint, New York: Macmillan, 1986), day 167.

38.1 Oswald Chambers, *Making All Things New* (Oswald Chambers Publications Association, Ltd., 1930), 25.

38.2 Ibid., 18.

38.3 J. P. de Caussade, "The Future," in *A Diary of Readings,* ed. John Baillie (1955; reprint, New York: Macmillan, 1986), day 22.

38.4 François Fénelon, *Christian Perfection* (New York: Harper & Row, 1947), 5.

38.5 A. W. Tozer, *The Pursuit of God* (Harrisburg, Pa.: Christian Publications, 1948), 31.

38.6 Jeanne Guyon, *Experiencing God through Prayer* (Springdale, Pa.: Whitaker House, 1984), 39.

38.7 Charles G. Finney, *Memoirs of Charles G. Finney* (Grand Rapids: Zondervan, 1989), 459.

39.1 Oswald Chambers, *Making All Things New* (Oswald Chambers Publications Association, Ltd., 1930), 72.

39.2 St. John of the Cross, "Support," in *A Diary of Readings,* ed. John Baillie (1955; reprint, New York: Macmillan, 1986), day 247.

39.3 Charles G. Finney, *Memoirs of Charles G.*

Finney (Grand Rapids: Zondervan, 1989), 457–458.

39.4 Ibid., 463.

39.5 J. Hudson Taylor, *Hudson Taylor's Legacy,* quoted in *Giant Steps,* ed. Warren W. Wiersbe (Grand Rapids: Baker, 1981), 178–179.

39.6 John Newton, *Letters of John Newton,* quoted in *Giant Steps,* ed. Warren W. Wiersbe (Grand Rapids: Baker, 1981), 69.

39.7 François Fénelon, *Christian Perfection* (New York: Harper & Row, 1947), 20-21.

40.1 Oswald Chambers, *Bringing Sons into Glory* (Oswald Chambers Publications Association, Ltd., 1943), 75.

40.2 Ibid., 56.

40.3 Oswald Chambers, *Making All Things New* (Oswald Chambers Publications Association, Ltd., 1930), 54.

40.4 Thomas à Kempis, *The Imitation of Christ,* quoted in *Giant Steps,* ed. Warren W. Wiersbe (Grand Rapids: Baker, 1981), 14.

40.5 François Fénelon, *Christian Perfection* (New York: Harper & Row, 1947), 4.

40.6 Ibid., 8.

40.7 Bernard of Clairvaux, "God's Rights," in *A*

Diary of Readings, ed. John Baillie (1955; reprint, New York: Macmillan, 1986), day 89.

41.1 Clement of Rome, in *Early Christian Writings* (New York: Dorset Press, 1986), 35–36.

41.2 Ibid., 41.

41.3 Alexander Whyte, quoted in *Giant Steps,* ed. Warren W. Wiersbe (Grand Rapids: Baker, 1981), 201.

41.4 Jeanne Guyon, *Madame Guyon, an Autobiography* (Chicago: Moody Press, n.d.), 264.

41.5 Andrew Murray, "Like Christ, In His Dependence on the Father," in *The Best of Andrew Murray* (Grand Rapids: Baker, 1990), 31.

41.6 George Matheson, *Rests by the River: Devotional Meditations,* quoted in *Giant Steps,* ed. Warren W. Wiersbe (Grand Rapids: Baker, 1981), 218–219.

41.7 Andrew Murray, *The True Vine* (Chicago: Moody Press, n.d.), 24–25.

42.1 The Didache, in *Early Christian Writings* (New York: Dorset Press, 1986), 235.

42.2 John Owen, "Not Yet to Die?" in *A Diary of Readings,* ed. John Baillie (1955; reprint, New York: Macmillan, 1986), day 25.

42.3 Johann Tauler, "Assurance," in *A Diary of*

Readings, ed. John Baillie (1955; reprint, New York: Macmillan, 1986), day 180.

42.4 John Owen, "This Peculiar Bitterness of the Cup," in *A Diary of Readings,* ed. John Baillie (1955; reprint, New York: Macmillan, 1986), day 322.

42.5 François Fénelon, *Christian Perfection* (New York: Harper & Row, 1947), 104.

42.6 Ibid., 104.

42.7 John Caird, "How to Prepare for Eternity," in *A Diary of Readings,* ed. John Baillie (1955; reprint, New York: Macmillan, 1986), day 138.

43.1 Barnabas, The Epistle of Barnabas, in *Early Christian Writings* (New York: Dorset Press, 1986), 220.

43.2 G. Campbell Morgan, *The Westminster Pulpit,* quoted in *Giant Steps,* ed. Warren W. Wiersbe (Grand Rapids: Baker, 1981), 271.

43.3 Oswald Chambers, *My Utmost for His Highest,* quoted in *Giant Steps,* ed. Warren W. Wiersbe (Grand Rapids: Baker, 1981), 314–315.

43.4 Dwight L. Moody, *The Best of Dwight L. Moody,* quoted in *Giant Steps,* ed. Warren W. Wiersbe (Grand Rapids: Baker, 1981), 212–213.

43.5 John Bunyan, "Thy Righteousness is in Heaven," in *A Diary of Readings,* ed. John Baillie

(1955; reprint, New York: Macmillan, 1986), day 63.

43.6 Oswald Chambers, *My Utmost for His Highest,* quoted in *Giant Steps,* ed. Warren W. Wiersbe (Grand Rapids: Baker, 1981), 315.

43.7 E. M. Bounds, *The Essentials of Prayer,* in *The Complete Works of E. M. Bounds* (Grand Rapids: Baker, 1990), 116.

44.1 W. R. Inge, "Hope," in *A Diary of Readings,* ed. John Baillie (1955; reprint, New York: Macmillan, 1986), day 19.

44.2 John Calvin, *Institutes of the Christian Religion,* quoted in *Giant Steps,* ed. Warren W. Wiersbe (Grand Rapids: Baker, 1981), 21.

44.3 Richard Baxter, "Per Ardua," in *A Diary of Readings,* ed. John Baillie (1955; reprint, New York: Macmillan, 1986), day 55.

44.4 Dietrich Bonhoeffer, *Letters and Papers from Prison,* rev. ed. (New York: Collier Books, 1972), 11.

44.5 John Henry Newman, *Parochial and Plain Sermons,* quoted in *Giant Steps,* ed. Warren W. Wiersbe (Grand Rapids: Baker, 1981), 85–86.

44.6 Dietrich Bonhoeffer, *Letters and Papers from Prison,* rev. ed. (New York: Collier Books, 1972), 12.

44.7 Andrew Murray, *With Christ in the School of Prayer*, in *The Best of Andrew Murray* (Grand Rapids: Baker, 1990), 19.

45.1 Augustine of Hippo, *The City of God* (New York: Image Book, Doubleday, 1958), 49.

45.2 George Matheson, *Rests by the River: Devotional Meditations*, quoted in *Giant Steps*, ed. Warren W. Wiersbe (Grand Rapids: Baker, 1981), 218.

45.3 Frederick William Faber, *Spiritual Conferences*, quoted in *Giant Steps*, ed. Warren W. Wiersbe (Grand Rapids: Baker, 1981), 111.

45.4 Jessie Penn-Lewis, *Power for Service* (Bristol, England: Overcomer Publications, n.d.), 25.

45.5 François Fénelon, *Christian Perfection* (New York: Harper & Row, 1947), 137.

45.6 J. Hudson Taylor, *Hudson Taylor's Legacy*, quoted in *Giant Steps*, ed. Warren W. Wiersbe (Grand Rapids: Baker, 1981), 174–175.

45.7 Andrew Murray, *The True Vine* (Chicago: Moody Press, n.d.), 50–51.

46.1 Sir John Seeley, "Christ's Object," in *A Diary of Readings*, ed. John Baillie (1955; reprint, New York: Macmillan, 1986), day 140.

46.2 George Macdonald, "Himself in His Dungeon," in *A Diary of Readings*, ed. John

Baillie (1955; reprint, New York: Macmillan, 1986), day 163.

46.3 Teresa of Avila, "The Way of Perfection," in *A Life of Prayer* (Portland, Oreg.: Multnomah, 1983), 221.

46.4 Andrew Murray, "Like Christ: In His Love," in *The Best of Andrew Murray* (Grand Rapids: Baker, 1990), 37.

46.5 Jeanne Guyon, *Madame Guyon, an Autobiography* (Chicago: Moody Press, n.d.), 42.

46.6 Ibid., 264.

46.7 François Fénelon, *Christian Perfection* (New York: Harper & Row, 1947), 205.

47.1 Andrew Murray, "Abide in Christ and in His Love," in *The Best of Andrew Murray* (Grand Rapids: Baker, 1990), 67.

47.2 Teresa of Avila, "The Way of Perfection," in *A Life of Prayer* (Portland, Oreg.: Multnomah, 1983), 222.

47.3 François Fénelon, *Christian Perfection* (New York: Harper & Row, 1947), 114–115.

47.4 Ignatius of Antioch, Letter to the Ephesians, in *Early Christian Writings* (New York: Dorset Press, 1986), 79–80.

47.5 Archibald C. Craig, "Envy," in *A Diary of*

Readings, ed. John Baillie (1955; reprint, New York: Macmillan, 1986), day 47.

47.6 Francis de Sales, "Opportunities of Grace," in *A Diary of Readings,* ed. John Baillie (1955; reprint, New York: Macmillan, 1986), day 122.

47.7 Jeanne Guyon, *Madame Guyon, an Autobiography* (Chicago: Moody, Press, n.d.), 156.

48.1 A. W. Tozer, *The Knowledge of the Holy* (New York: Harper & Row, 1961), 110.

48.2 E. M. Bounds, *The Essentials of Prayer,* in *The Complete Works of E. M. Bounds* (Grand Rapids: Baker, 1990), 87.

48.3 Francis of Assisi, "Admonition" in *Through the Years with Francis of Assisi* (New York: Image Book, Doubleday, 1987), 87.

48.4 Barnabas, The Epistle of Barnabas, in *Early Christian Writings* (New York: Dorset Press, 1986), 217.

48.5 Andrew Murray, "Like Christ: In Forgiving," in *The Best of Andrew Murray* (Grand Rapids: Baker, 1990), 51.

48.6 Jeanne Guyon, *Madame Guyon, an Autobiography* (Chicago: Moody Press, n.d.), 44.

48.7 Father Congreve, "Levi Made Him a Great Feast," in *A Diary of Readings,* ed. John Baillie

(1955; reprint, New York: Macmillan, 1986), day 266.

49.1 Clement of Rome, The First Epistle of Clement, in *Early Christian Writings* (New York: Dorset Press, 1986), 49.

49.2 Ibid., 50.

49.3 Francis of Assisi, "Letter to a Minister," in *Through the Years with Francis of Assisi* (New York: Image Book, Doubleday, 1987), 24.

49.4 Samuel Johnson, "Forgiveness," in *A Diary of Readings,* ed. John Baillie (1955; reprint, New York: Macmillan, 1986), day 176.

49.5 Andrew Murray, "Like Christ: In Forgiving," in *The Best of Andrew Murray* (Grand Rapids: Baker, 1990), 52.

49.6 William Temple, "The Conditions of Forgiveness," in *A Diary of Readings,* ed. John Baillie (1955; reprint, New York: Macmillan, 1986), day 70.

49.7 Alexander Whyte, "Where to find God," in *A Diary of Readings,* ed. John Baillie (1955; reprint, New York: Macmillan, 1986), day 16.

50.1 Henri-Frédéric Amiel, "Every Life a Profession of Faith," in *A Diary of Readings,* ed. John Baillie (1955; reprint, New York: Macmillan, 1986), day 158.

50.2 Andrew Murray, *Working for God*, in *The Best of Andrew Murray* (Grand Rapids: Baker, 1990), 181.

50.3 Phillips Brooks, *Sermons*, quoted in *Giant Steps*, ed. Warren W. Wiersbe (Grand Rapids: Baker, 1981), 199.

50.4 J. Stuart Holden, *A Voice for God*, quoted in *Giant Steps*, ed. Warren W. Wiersbe (Grand Rapids: Baker, 1981), 320–321.

50.5 François Fénelon, *Christian Perfection* (New York: Harper & Row, 1947), 21.

50.6 Henri-Frédéric Amiel, "Every Life a Profession of Faith," in *A Diary of Readings*, ed. John Baillie (1955; reprint, New York: Macmillan, 1986), day 158.

50.7 Hannah Whitall Smith, *The Christian's Secret of a Happy Life* (Old Tappan, N.J.: Revell, 1952), 185.

51.1 Robert S. Candlish, "Sermons from the late Robert S. Candlish," in *Giant Steps*, ed. Warren W. Wiersbe (Grand Rapids: Baker, 1981), 89.

51.2 Charles G. Finney, *Memoirs of Charles G. Finney* (Grand Rapids: Zondervan, 1989), 28.

51.3 E. M. Bounds, *The Essentials of Prayer*, in *The Complete Works of E. M. Bounds* (Grand Rapids: Baker, 1990), 142.

51.4 Teresa of Avila, "The Way of Perfection," in *A Life of Prayer* (Portland, Oreg.: Multnomah, 1983), 221.

51.5 Andrew Murray, *The True Vine* (Chicago: Moody Press, n.d.), 51–52.

51.6 Jessie Penn-Lewis, *Power for Service* (Bristol, England: Overcomer Publications, n.d.), 21.

51.7 Hannah Whitall Smith, *The Christian's Secret of a Happy Life* (Old Tappan, N.J.: Revell, 1952), 87.

52.1 Charles G. Finney, *Memoirs of Charles G. Finney* (Grand Rapids: Zondervan, 1989), 138.

52.2 William Law, *A Serious Call to a Devout and Holy Life* (E. P. Dutton, 1908), 294.

52.3 Charles G. Finney, *Memoirs of Charles G. Finney* (Grand Rapids: Zondervan, 1989), 139.

52.4 E. M. Bounds, *The Essentials of Prayer,* in *The Complete Works of E. M. Bounds* (Grand Rapids: Baker, 1990), 141.

52.5 Andrew Murray, "Paul, a Pattern of Prayer," in *The Best of Andrew Murray* (Grand Rapids: Baker, 1990), 129.

52.6 Ibid.

52.7 Ignatius of Antioch, *Letter to the Ephesians,* in *Early Christian Writings* (New York: Dorset Press, 1986), 78–79.

Discover hope for recovery through these Tyndale products:

THE BIBLE PROMISE LIFE RECOVERY DEVOLUTIONAL   0-8423-3810-1
THE TWELVE STEP LIFE RECOVERY DEVOTIONAL   0-8423-4753-4
David Stoop, Ph.D., and Stephen Arterburn, M.Ed.

WHEN IT'S HARD TO TRUST   0-8423-7955-X
WHEN WE CAN'T TALK ANYMORE   0-8423-7987-8
Steve Wilke and Dave and Neta Jackson

The Life Recovery Bible
Published for those in recovery, this Bible offers divine wisdom and hope for healing through God's Son, Jesus Christ. It features twelve-step recovery devotionals and numerous recovery notes. Available in *The Living Bible* version, hardcover and softcover.